A COLLECTOR'S HANDBOOK
Miniature Perfume
Minis, Mates and More
BOTTLES

AVANT L'AMOUR

Jeri Lyn Ringblum

77 Lower Valley Road, Atglen, PA 19310

Library of Congress Cataloging-in-Publication Data

Ringblum, Jeri Lyn.
    A collector's handbook of miniature perfume bottles : A
Schiffer book for collectors / Jeri Lyn Ringblum.
        p. cm.
    Includes bibliographical references and index.
    ISBN 0-7643-0038-5 (paper)
    1. Perfumes--Collectors and collecting. 2. Perfume
paraphernalia--Collectors and collecting. I. Title.
TP983.R477   1996
668'.54--dc20   96-6012
                                                        CIP

ISBN: 0-7643-0038-5
Printed in Hong Kong

Published by Schiffer Publishing Ltd.
77 Lower Valley Road
Atglen, PA 19310
Please write for a free catalog.
This book may be purchased from
the publisher.
Please include $2.95 for shipping.
Try your bookstore first.

To all whom I love and hold dear.
My Creator
———— *Rosemary Murray, MS, LCSW* ————
Oleg and Larisa Zemlyanko
My entire Family

Acknowledgments

I want to say a heartfelt thanks to all those who gave so generously in the creation of this book. It is so true that "no man is an island," and without the patience and contributions of others this book would not exist as it does. Their contributions and hard work were done, not for me, but through me, so that you may enjoy and learn about the world of fragrance and its creation.

Thank you to my parents Margaret Ringblum and Roger Sowell for their unconditional love, belief, and support in helping me to realize my dream. To Rick and Terry Blackwell, Crystal Blackwell, Kelly Anderson, Patrick Anderson, David and Gloria Ringblum, Jason and Wendy Phillips, Derrick Sowell, Helen Farnsworth, Barbara Moskowitz, Marian Bendeth, Dr. and Mrs. Kneeland, Beth Workman, Rosemary Hubbard, Mary Musser, Christy Wood, Don LaCoss, Leota McClendon, Larry and Nancy Beasley, Randy and Candi Sowell, and Schiffer Publishing and team members.

A standing ovation goes to the following participating companies and individuals whose commitment to excellence in public service is exemplary in any industry.

Alfred Dunhill Limited: Howard S. Smith, Archive Controller
Aramis Inc.: Patrick Morris, Public Relations
Atlantis International, Ltd.: Christine Famighetti, Marketing Manager
Avon Products, Inc.: Amy Walton, Public Relations
Benetton Cosmetics Corporation: Lori Singer, Director of Marketing
Bijan Fragrances: Brett Neubig, Director of Corporate
   Communications
Caesar's World Marketing: Gena Ferrer, Asst. Vice President, Mkt.
Calvin Klein Cosmetics: Marie Stuart, Consumer Affairs
Cassini Parfums, Ltd.: Marianne Nestor, President
Christian Dior: Veronica Post, Consumer Affairs
Clarins USA Inc.: Tina Haskins, Consumer Relations Specialist
Coty: Jane Schraff, Consumer Relations
Erox Corp.: Michael V. Stern, Vice President, Marketing & Sales
Fragrance Marketing Group, Inc.: Michelle Rabunski, Brand
   Manager

French Fragrances, Inc.: Les Parfums Salvador Dali & Parfums Aubusson: Gretchen Cuzydlo, Sr. VP Marketing

Frances Rothschild, Inc.: Cherylann Biel, Customer Service

Gale Hayman Beverly Hills: Nadine Johnson

Giorgio Beverly Hills: Daphne Ann Sheridan Bass, General Counsel

Groupe Inter Parfums: Anne Duboscq, Chef de Produits

Guerlain, Inc.: Dana Glazer, Director of Public Relations

Holzman & Stephanie: Esther R. Holzman, Owner

Jean Patou, Inc.: Marie Joyce, Customer Relations

Lippens Inc. Int'l: Fabienne Chiasson, Products Manager Brands Developement

Madeleine Mono, Ltd.: Madeleine Mono, President

Marilyn Miglin, Inc.: Pam Lassers, Vice President

Merle Norman Cosmetics: Sallie Cereghetti, Director Corporate Public Relations

Masson Agencies, Ltd.; Quebec, Canada: Jacques Masson, President

Nordstrom, Inc.: Paula Stanley, Public Affairs Coordinator

Parfums Givenchy, Inc.: Isabelle de Munnick, Assistant Manager Marketing & Public Relations

Parfums Rochas: Marie Joyce, Customer Relations

Parlux Fragrances: Andrea Koons, Marketing Manager

Perfumes of Hawaii by Langer: David N. Langer, President

Revlon: Denise Quattrochi, Publicity Assistant

Richard Barrie Fragrances, Maria Hannon, Marketing Coordinator

Riviera Concepts Inc.: Pamela Kennedy, Public Relations Coordinator

Tiffany & Co.: Kimberly Brewer

Victoria's Secret: Regina Stought

Zenue, Division of Hydrotech Laboratories: Jennifer Hamilton

Contents

Preface

This book is a compilation of years of inspiration, intuition, dedication, and hard work. Not just on my part—but on the part of all who are involved in the creation of a fragrance.

The creation of any fragrance first originates in the imagination. It can present itself in many ways. It can come as an intuition, perhaps something from a dream. It can arise from an inspiration so powerful that it moved the creator to give it life. Many stories of inspiration can be found in the majestic influence of nature or a moment witnessed of passion so delicate, so profound, that it could not be ignored. It can also arise in of honor of someone admired and cherished. Whatever the motivation, the creation of any fragrance, from the fragrance itself to its packaging, is a visual presentation of the human imagination. Jacques Courtin-Clarins put it most eloquently when he said, "Sometimes the heart sees what the eye cannot."

Introduction

As essential as any historical force, the history of fragrance and its use has recorded financial status and trends, medical and religious practices, cultural and societal barriers, personal etiquette and habits, and even the shifting likes and dislikes in art.

Dating back to a time still unknown, the use of fragrance, in any form, was used as a tool for identifying, idealizing, and reinforcing these cultural standards and rituals. Remaining unchallenged, the same still holds true today to some degree although modern fragrances and packagings are designed to satisfy the interests and demands of a broader audience to include people from all walks of life.

Before the 19th century, scents and fragrances were created to appease Gods, royalty, and aristocracy. As an intrinsic part of any fashionable and refined lifestyle, perfume was used as a symbol of wealth and luxury. Perfume was used to establish boundaries between classes and cultures, and idealized a time of frivolous and carefree lifestyles in the single minded pursuit of pleasure. Because all areas of life were influenced, and perhaps to a certain extent even defined, by the use of scents and fragrances, artisans and craftsmen had to refine and improve their work on containers to satisfy the public's ever grow-ing demand. This demand for fragrances "forced" artisans and crafts-men to become more creative and innovative in their designs of con-tainers.

In addition to self-idealizing and self-adornment, perfume and scents played vital roles in religious ceremonies and medical practices. It was common for physician's healing practices to include the use of herbal remedies, scented ointments, and perfumed water to cure the ills of the time. For example, the use of distilled rose water was admin-istered internally as a medicine for strengthening an ailing heart. The use of nature's bounty is still widely practiced, although it has sepa-rated itself from what we consider modern medicine and is today known as alternative medicine.

Before Christ's time, religious leaders made frequent, pleading offerings of fragrant smoke to appease an upset god or to hold favor, even in times of good. This practice was not limited to one religion or spiritual belief system. In Taoism, for example, a festival is held every year to honor the Goddess of Flowers, Faah Seen. In this elaborate ceremony, flowers and their extractions are meticulously prepared and used strategically in the request for abundance.

But today the emphasis in on the ephemeral. New and better fragrance needs and desires are in constant demand. We have gained a vast amount of knowledge about the workings of nature and have become more interested in the psychology and artistic aspects of fragrances. Each part or process in the creation of a fragrance adds to the history recording process no matter how short lived, from the fragrance itself, to its packaging.

There are certain standard elements needed to create a fragrance. First, the fragrance name, while not always difficult to come by, is always directly connected to the fragrance. The name must convey the creator's intention or motivation. The fragrance name gives the fragrance its unique identity and helps to establish the fragrance's philosophy.

The fragrance itself, or *juice*, is especially important today. An entire field of study devoted to the psychology of fragrance gives us new insight on the type of fragrance or scent that most appeal to a particular population in any part of the world. This has been made easier with the new technologies and abilities in synthesizing scents.

And last but not least, the bottle and packaging, whether envisioned by the creator or another artisan, is designed to reflect the contents within. This is easy to identify, although not all are so simple, when we spy a fragrance bottle and package designed with floral motif. This visual presentation gives us a message as to what we can expect from the fragrance.

Although these fragrances, bottles, and their packaging may appear simple or plain, they still represent the workings of the imagination. They give us an opportunity to appreciate and participate in the diversity of nature and cultural backgrounds other than our own. Being able to participate in such diversity makes perfume and scent bottle collecting an exciting and personally rewarding adventure.

Disclaimers

This book is intended as a guide to understanding both fragrance content and the inspiration within the creation of a fragrance, the bottle, and its packaging. A challenging project, the information contained within this book has been presented as accurately as possible.

Included is a category is referred to as "Other." The fragrances listed under this category are not necessarily found in miniature or sample sizes nor do they represent the entire fragrance line, but are listed as a courtesy to the reader to help in identifying fragrances within a family. Readers are encouraged to familiarize themselves with these fragrance families.

The CPG, or Collector's Price Guide, is based on a Mid-west, four-state, geographical area and does not represent "retail" prices or other pricing practices found in other areas of the United States. The CPG is intended to be used as a guideline only. You will also find photos of *contemporary* fragrances shown that do not include packaging; the CPG has been based on a WITH BOX/IN MINT CONDITION status.

Some fragrances represented in this book are sold exclusively as "gift sets" or not sold individually at any time by the originating company. They are most commonly intended as "Gift With Purchase" or for promotional purposes only.

There are many ways in which a fragrance company will distribute its fragrance, i.e., sample vial or uniquely designed bottles for different fragrance concentrations. Not all bottles shown in this book are replicas of the larger, original bottle design and are not represented to be so. The use of stock or sample bottles are shown as a courtesy to aide the reader in familiarizing themselves with a fragrance.

About Fragrances

Fragrance Concentrations

Parfum: The most concentrated and longest lasting form of fragrance.
Eau de Parfum: The base is slightly modified and less concentrated than perfume.
Eau de Toilette: Lighter in concentration and fresher.
Eau de Cologne: The lightest fragrance concentration.

Structure of a Fragrance

Top Notes: First impression of a fragrance. This part of the fragrance lasts only for a few moments.
Middle (heart) Notes: A blend of all the different notes. Middle notes usually linger for several hours.
Base (bottom) Notes: Fixed notes that create a longer lasting scent, sometimes lasting for several days.

Fragrance Definitions

Absolutes: Natural plant extractions.
Accords: Blended combinations of a variety of single notes.
Aldehyde: Chemical process that allows the perfumer to use new notes—odor effect of floral and woody tones.
Aromatic: Notes of basil, tarragon, thyme.
Bouquet: Mixture of floral notes.
Chypre: Chapy fragrances with leathery, woody, mossy, and animal notes.
Fougère: Herbaceous lavender notes atop a mossy foundation.
Fresh: A term used to reflect an impression of a fragrance using citrus, green, and floral notes.
Green: Scents that reflect grass and leaves.
Herbaceous: Herbs such as mugwort, sage, and rosemary.
Oriental: Exotic and mystery-like scents reminiscent of the Far East. These include exotic flowers and spices.

Powdery: The use of mosses, woods, and sweet elements create a powdery olfactory effect.

Sensual: Animal and exotic floral notes help create this fragrance effect.

Spicy: Tropical flowers and spices.

Sweet: Vanilla.

Raw Ingredients Used in Fragrances

Animal Notes: Ambergris, Civet, Musk

Barks: Birch, Cinnamon

Citrus: Lemon, Limes, Orange

Flowers: Jasmine, Narcissus, Rose

Fruits: Apple, Berries, Plum

Gums: Balsams, Benzoin, Galbanum

Gum Resins: Frankincense, Myrrh, Opoponax

Leaves: Patchouli, Sage

Mosses: Oakmoss

Rhizomes: Iris

Roots: Vetiver

Seeds: Cardamon, Coriander

Spices: Cinnamon, Cloves, Nutmeg

Buying Tips

From Mother to Daughter—it seems only natural that way. Mothers pass on to their daughters what they consider to be precious and splendid. Among these heirlooms, perfume and scent bottles can be found. And in Barbara Moskowitz's case, it was an entire store of perfume and scent bottles. Barbara's mother, Iris Fields, owned and operated Iris Fields Antiques for a number of years, eventually specializing in scent and perfume bottles. Barbara Moskowitz has offered ten bottle buying tips that can help you in that moment of indecision.

Ten Tips for Buying Bottles...

1. Hold the bottle in your hands without looking at it and rely on your sense of touch to feel chips or nicks.
2. Check the stopper. If you see a number, make sure it matches the number on the base. Very good manufacturers custom fit the stopper the to base.
3. Don't pass up a bottle if it does have a nick or chip because if you love it, that is all that counts. Besides, a glass man may be able to repair it.
4. Examine the stopper to see if it is loose or do you have to force it closed. Someone may have lost the original stopper and replaced it.
5. Commercial bottles have more value with their boxes. However, do not pass up a bottle in which the box has a rip or stain. Remember it may have been through three different hands and be fifty or sixty years old.
6. If a bottle has perfume residue, I would recommend leaving it as opposed to cleaning it. Cleaning it may damage the label or bottle itself and I feel it looks more romantic with the original fragrance.

7. If the bottle looks too new and it is in a "perfect" box—examine it carefully! A few beautiful bottles have been reissued. Do not pay the price of an older (original) bottle when it is a newer reissue. There are beautiful reissues which are much more affordable than the originals. I personally would not pass on them. Example: Jean Patou, Guerlain, and Egyptian bottles—all have original bottles with reissues.
8. Buy bottles that have labels. I find that a bottle that says Baccarat with no label isn't exciting unless it's a colored glass or unusual shape. Finding labels can be very difficult.
9. If you see a base with no stopper which is rare, i.e. Lalique, Dior, Baccarat, or older Schapperellis, you can run an advertisement and may find someone who kept the stopper in hopes of finding a base or can lead you in a direction which may land you that splendid stopper you are looking for. My advice to all my clients—if they break a bottle, keep the good part and I am always willing to help in "matchmaking" customers.
10. Don't pass on a bottle because of the price. It may be rare to find and you may never come across it again! *Most Importantly*: "If you LOVE a bottle BUY IT! It will be valuable simply because you love it!"

Barbara Moskowitz
Iris Fields Antiques
60 N. Federal Highway
Dania, Florida 33004.

Fragrance Tips

Marian Bendeth, of Sixth Scents, is a Fragrance Specialist who consults with the Fragrance Industry as well as the public. She specializes in fragrance wardrobing and works with over five hundred (500) prestige lines and appropriates them based on body chemistry, personality, psychology, and lifestyle.

Fragrance Tips from Marian Bendeth...

As a Fragrance Specialist, I am often asked "What is the mystery of fragrance"? How does one define a feeling or mood evoked which is subjective to say the least!

The history and mystery of perfume has affected humankind for thousands of years. It has left its mark on religions, created commerce, and at one time it actually surpassed currency and precious gems as the ultimate status symbol.

The twentieth century has offered us a plethora of scents in which to choose from. The usage of fragrance has now become an art form. The psychology of smell or aromachology plays an important role in the application of certain scents. Our decisions in purchasing are now based on: 1) How does the fragrance make me feel when I wear it? and 2) How do I wish others to perceive me? Bear in mind, these thought processes are conducted on a subliminal level and the long-term effects are stored in the brain where the memory function will store these emotions.

We all, at one time or another, have made mental assumptions on others around us based on their fragrance preferences. These positive or negative evaluations colour our view of individuals, especially in a working environment.

There are three basic types of fragrances: 1) Sport Scents, 2) Day/Corporate Scents, and 3) Evening Scents. Evening scents are usually more pungent than the other two classifications and should not be worn in the workplace.

To ascertain which fragrances best suit your body chemistry and lifestyle, it is important to test your scents on the pulse points. Do not rub your wrists together as this will bruise the blending process. The scent should remain after one hour or more. You should also surmise whether the scent is appropriate for your activity, but most importantly, the fragrance should delight, enhance, and reflect your self-esteem.

Marian Bendeth, Fragrance Specialist
Sixth Scents
3555 Don Mills Road Suite 6
Willowdale, Ontario, Canada M2H 3N3.

ADOLFO
Adolfo Sardina

Adolfo® for Women
Launch Date: 1978
Fragrance Type: Eau de Toilette: Floral
Pictured Size: .25oz.
Dimensions: 2" h x 1-3/8" w
CPG: $6.00

Adolfo Classic Gentlemen®
Launch Date: 1981
Fragrance Type: Eau de Toilette: Chypre
Pictured Size: .25oz.
Dimensions: 2" h x 1-1/2" w
CPG: $5.00

ADRIENNE VITTADINI
Adrienne Vittadini

AV® PARFUM
Launch Date: 1995
Fragrance Type: Eau de Parfum: Floral bouquet of freesia, ylang-ylang, Rose de Mai, and white jasmine. Additional notes are musk, sandalwood, and oakmoss.
Bottle Design: Bottle design by world famous Pierre Dinand.
Pictured Size: .25oz.
Dimensions: 2" h x 1-1/2" w
CPG: $22.00 (Gift set, 1995)

ALAIN DELON
Alain Delon, Paris-Geneve

Iquitos®
Launch Date: 1987
Fragrance Type: Eau de Toilette: Chypre-Woody.
Package Design: "Oriental take-out" fashioned red container.
Pictured Size: .17oz.
Dimensions: 2" h x 1-1/2" w
CPG: $5.00

Other Alain Delon Fragrances

Alain Delon®
Launch Date: 1980
Fragrance Type: Fougère: Woody and ambered.

Alain Delon Plus®
Launch Date: 1987
Fragrance Type: Fougère: Woody and ambered.

ALBERT NIPON
Albert Nipon Fragrances

Albert Nipon®
Launch Date: c1985
Fragrance Type: Perfume: Fruity and citrusy top notes with a heart of spicy, floral notes and base notes that are sweet, powdery, and mossy.
Pictured Size: .25oz.
Dimensions: 1-1/8" h x 1-1/2" w
CPG: $8.00

Fun Facts
On Carnations
Carnations are considered to be valuable for their skin revitalizing and premature aging properties.

ALBERTA FERRETTI

Femina®
Launch Date: 1993
Fragrance Type: Eau de Parfum: Fresh-Floral.
Pictured Size: .25oz.
Dimensions: 2-1/4" h x 1-3/8" w
CPG: $9.00

ALEXANDRA DE MARKOFF
Revlon, Inc.

No Regrets®
"...BECAUSE LIFE IS TOO SHORT"
Launch Date: September, 1994
Fragrance Type: Parfum: Alexandra de Markoff's signature fragrance is a complex white floral with woody, fruity, and spicy notes that give this fragrance its sophistication and élan.
Bottle Design: *No Regrets* bottles are true "conversation pieces." The "Love" series of bottles are decorated with age old insights about loving while the "Life" series contains some of literature's great truisms about living. Each bottle underscores interesting things that happen to women with *No Regrets*.
Package Design: Gold packaging decorated with age old insights.
Pictured Size: .12oz.
Dimensions: 3-1/8" h x 3/4" w
CPG: $25.00

Other Alexandra de Markoff Fragrances

Alexandra®
Launch Date: 1979

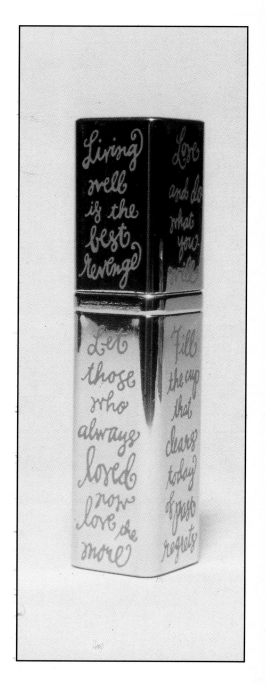

Love is merely a madness
Gather ye rosebuds while ye may
She who has never loved has never lived
No time like the present
I can resist everything except temptation
All this and heaven too
Oh come with me and be my love
Living well is the best revenge
Let those who always loved now love the more
Love and do what you will
No regrets in life - No regrets in love
Fill the cup that clears today of past regrets

ALFRED SUNG
Riviera Concepts Inc.

E•n•c•o•r•e®

Launch Date: September, 1990

Fragrance Type: Perfume: This elegant floriental fragrance envelops the wearer in a soft cloud of ultra-femininity. The top note is a diffusive floral accord that is both distinctive and comfortable. A sparkling hint of tangerine enhances the freshness of the initial burst. The mid notes resonate with only the richest of beautiful florals. Mousse de Chine weaves throughout the floralcy, adding fullness and depth. The tenacious residual is a harmonious blend of precious woods such as sandalwood and patchouli with exotics encens (qualities). Subtle hints of vanilla and musk notes provide the warm, romantic trailing effect of this classic creation.

Bottle Design: As all great bottles, such as *SUNG*, are designed by Pierre Dinand, history repeats itself with *E•N•C•O•R•E*. This refined, romantic flacon reflects the woman who wears *E•N•C•O•R•E*. The soft curves, the shiny silver accent, the ultra-feminine frosted shoulders, the sophisticated, sculpted stopper.

Package Design: The magical harmony of the subtle-shaped bottle and precious package presentation symbolize romance. The marriage of colors - marble gray, radiant red and striking silver create a look of luxury. The coffret, a true expression of femininity, surrounds the delicate cognac color perfume.

Pictured Size: .14oz. (Deluxe Miniature Size)

Dimensions: 1-1/4" h x 1-1/2" w

CPG: $9.00

Alfred Sung Forever®
"Forever Changing. Forever the same."
Launch Date: June, 1995
Fragrance Type: Perfume: *Alfred Sung Forever* is a rhapsody of florals designed to evolve and caress the feminine senses. *Alfred Sung Forever* opens with Mirabelle plum, tayberry, and pink peony buds. It blossoms into a beautiful heart of yellow freesia, paperwhite narcisse, and Damask rose. As the fresh River Rock accord flows throughout the fragrance, lily-of-the-valley, yellow bell mahonia, sandalwood, and amber perfectly balance the breezy floral bouquet. (The perfumer, Dragoco. River Rock Accord-Aura Scent - a transparent scent impression interwoven into the fragrance reminiscent of water flowing endlessly over rocks. Aura Scent™ technology brings us closer to nature.)
Bottle Design: Wanting a specific color for the glass along with the silver cap reflecting softness and femininity, Alfred Sung designed the bottle working with Pierre Dinand on the mechanics of the flacon. A celadon green collection of soft, smooth fluid shapes embrace the floral composition of the fragrance.
Package Design: The soft silhouettes reflect the timeless elegance of the box.
Pictured Size: .17oz. (Deluxe Miniature Size)
Dimensions: 2-1/4" h x 3/4" w
CPG: $6.00

SUNG®
"The essence of style."
Launch Date: June, 1988
Fragrance Type: Perfume: This classic, white floral bouquet commences with a highly diffusive top note of sparkling citrus notes entwined with green floral nuances. The heart notes are a full-bodied blend of beautiful feminine florals, highlighting jasmine, iris, and muguet white flowers. A delicately fruity floral note of osmanthus weaves throughout the fragrance and lends a feeling of classic distinction. Fleur d'oranger rounds out the floralcy and leads into the tenacious residual note. Subtle musk notes and precious woods add depth and richness to this timeless creation.
Bottle Design: Pierre Dinand and Alfred SUNG fused their creativity in the designing of SUNG's first fragrance bottle collection. The *SUNG* fashion philosophy of timeless, classic and uncomplicated lines is reflected in the exquisitely designed bottle. Smooth, crystal clear and symmetrical, each perfume bottle is hand made in France from a single, carefully sculptured mold and individually inspected for perfection. To contrast the elegant

SUNG glass bottle is a glossy, black nylon accent made in England. Each mold is hand built and hand polished to ensure a perfect fit and high luster finish.

Package Design: The packaging of the signature perfumes is delicately processed in France using high gloss over wraps in three striking colors: platinum silver, black and white. Each piece is masterfully affixed by hand to create an elegantly hand made perfume box.

Pictured Size: .14oz. (Deluxe Miniature Size)
Dimensions: 1-3/4" h x 1-1/4" w
CPG: $15.00

SUNG® Homme

Launch Date: September, 1988
Fragrance Type: Eau de Toilette: This rich refined fragrance has a unique composition. It begins with a blend of crisp citrus top notes entwined with bold natural aromatic notes of galbanum, laurel nobile, and petitgrain. Harmonized by warm herbaceous heart notes and rich spices, Sung Homme is a distinctive scent with subtle persistence. The vitality of warm woody scents of vetiver, sandalwood, and patchouli create the base notes. Velvety oakmoss and sensual musk notes complete the tenacious residual of this intriguing classic scent. The fragrance color, hues of blue, establishes uniqueness of the sophisticated scent.

Bottle Design: The Sung Homme glass bottle echoes that of the Sung by Alfred Sung maintaining the smooth, crystal clear, symmetrical bottle. The bottle was created by Pierre Dinand and Alfred Sung. Hand made in France, each bottle is individually inspected for perfection.

Package Design: To manifest the masculine Sung Homme look, the package is masterfully processed in matte black complemented by a high gloss finish, completed with platinum silver trim.

Pictured Size: .20oz. (Deluxe Miniature Size)
Dimensions: 1-1/2" h x 1" w
CPG: $9.00

ANIMALE
Parlux Fragrances, Inc.

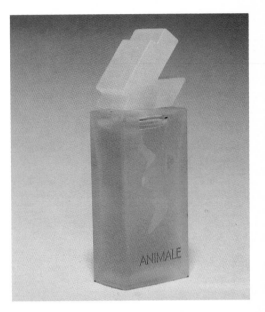

Animale® for Women
"Silently Seductive"
Launch Date: 1987
Fragrance Type: Eau de Parfum: Floral-Chypre.
Bottle Design: Lightning bolt cap atop a frosted
bottle etched with lightning bolt.
Package Design: Geometric graphics in teal green
with purple and orange accents.
Pictured Size: .17oz.
Dimensions: 2-3/8" h x 3/4" w
CPG: $11.00

Animale® for Men
"Pure Instinct"
Launch Date: 1993
Fragrance Type: Eau de Toilette: Modern
aromatic.
Bottle Design: A black granite-specked design
with signature lightning bolt.
Package Design: Black granite-specked with bold
red-orange and teal embossed lightning bolt.
Pictured Size: .17oz.
Dimensions: 2" h x 1" w
CPG: $8.00

Animale Animale® for Women
"Wildly Exotic"
Launch Date: 1994
Fragrance Type: Eau de Parfum: Fruity-floral, oriental.
Bottle Design: Lightning bolt cap atop a frosted bottle etched with lightning bolt.
Pictured Size: .17oz.
Dimensions: 2-3/8" h x 3/4" w
CPG: $10.00

Fun Facts
on Anne Klein
Noted New York fashion designer.

ANNE KLEIN

Anne Klein®
Launch Date: 1984 (Discontinued)
Fragrance Type: Parfum: Floral: Bergamot, hyacinth, mandarin, jasmine, Bulgarian rose, ylang-ylang, vetiver, sandalwood, and musk.
Pictured Size: .125oz.
Dimensions: 1" h x 1-1/2" w
CPG: $5.00

Anne Klein 11®

Launch Date: 1985 (Discontinued)
Fragrance Type: Parfum: Oriental-Amber: Vanilla,
amber, incense, oppopax, civet, oakmoss, exotic
woods, spices, tangerine, lilies, jasmine, orange
flower, peach, and apricot.
Pictured Size: .125oz.
Dimensions: 2-3/4" h x 1" w
CPG: $5.00

Other Anne Klein Fragrances

Blazer®

Launch Date: Prior 1984 (Discontinued)
Fragrance Type: Parfum: Fresh, citrusy top notes
blended with fruits, spices, and floral middle
notes. Base notes are powdery and feminine.
Bottle Design: Lion logo label was designed for
Anne Klein's astrological sign.

ARAMIS
Estee Lauder, Inc.

New West Skinscent® For Her

Launch Date: Fall, 1989
Fragrance Type: This fragrance is a fresh floral
fragrance with fruity and woody accords. Energizing bright top note combines the clarity of an
ozonic accord sparkling with florals. Accents are
crisply green, freshly fruity, and brightly citrus.
Brisk herbaceous elements reinforce the intriguing
airy yet tantalizingly feminine theme. Warmth
builds as mid notes emerge from the fruitiness of
plum, the spiciness of pimento and clove and rich
florals blended with woodiness of orris. The
background lingers the log accord of precious
wood notes merging with a sensuous touch of
oakmoss, amber, tonka, and musk.
Pictured Size: .25oz.
Dimensions: 2-1/4" h x 1" w
CPG: $10.00

Other Aramis Fragrances

Aramis®
Launch Date: 1964
Fragrance Type: Cologne

Aramis 900®
Launch Date: 1973
Fragrance Type: Herbal Cologne

Devin®
Launch Date: 1978
Fragrance Type: Country Cologne

New West Skinscent® For Him
Launch Date: 1988
Fragrance Type: Skinscent

THE COLLECTION
CREATED BY ARAMIS

AUBUSSON
Daniel Aubusson
Parfums Aubusson, Paris

Histoire d' Amour®
Launch Date: 1984
Fragrance Type: Parfum: Chypre-Floral: Citrus
top note imparts a significant let to the fragrances
composition.
Bottle Design: Spherical glass with floral design.
Top is half-folded bloomed flower.
Pictured Size: .25oz.
Dimensions: 2" h x 1-1/4" w
CPG: $5.00

28

25"®
Launch Date: Late, 1994
Fragrance Type: Parfum: A bouquet of white and
yellow flowers, explosion of colors, a real mosaic
with millions of reflections. A modern harmony,
completely new, reunites the elegance of cyclamen,
muguets, tuberose, white jasmine, and junguillos.

Aubusson® Homme
Launch Date: 1992
Fragrance Type: Eau de Toilette: The core
consists of an accord of masculine floral notes.
Abundant woody notes coated with sweet balsamic
notes.

Desirade®
Launch Date: 1990
Fragrance Type: Parfum: Floral-Semi-oriental.
Vivid citrus top note enhanced by sparkling aide
vdis.

Fun Facts	
on Cinnamon Bark	
Also used on the skin to help heal cuts and scrapes.	

AUVERGNE

After Five®
Launch Date: c1937
Fragrance Type: Perfume
Pictured Size: .03oz.
Dimensions: 1" h x 1/2" w
PG: $15.00 - $18.00

AVON PRODUCTS, INC.

Far Away®
Launch Date: September, 1994
Fragrance Type: Parfum: A complex floral oriental
fragrance developed for women all over the world.
It's designed to elicit a sense of a momentary
retreat to a private place, far away within one's
daydreams, where a busy woman can enjoy a
sense of calm. An inviting, lush introduction of
freesia, jasmine, and violet leaf comprises the top
note. The jewel of the middle note is karo
karounde, a West African flower related to the
gardenia. Vanilla bean absolute, velvety sandalwood, and musk make up the finishing under
notes.

Bottle Design: A frosted glass bottle, in the form of an interlocking yin-yang symbol, is dramatized by a cap of pearlized fuchsia and black. A black tassel is draped over the bottle's neck.
Package Design: The elegantly embossed cream colored carton features a fuchsia and black yin-yang symbol highlighted with a golden tassel.
Pictured Size: .125oz.
Dimensions: 1-1/2" h x 1-3/4" w
CPG: $12.00

AZZARO
Loris Azzaro
Loris Azzaro Parfums
Lippens Inc. International

Azzaro® Pour Homme
Launch Date: 1978
Fragrance Type: Eau de Toilette: An unconventional but harmonious mixture of fresh herbal essences, lavender, and spicy, woody overtones with musk and ambergris.
Pictured Size: .24oz.
Dimensions: 2-1/8" h x 1-3/8" w
CPG: $5.00

Azzaro 9®
Launch: 1984
Fragrance Type: Eau de Toilette: Exotic florals.
Pictured Size: .17oz.
Dimensions: 2" h x 1-3/4" w
CPG: $7.00

oh la la®
Launch Date: 1993
Fragrance Type: Eau de Parfum: Floriental: A perfect harmony of brilliance and tenderness, it is distinguished by a bold, mischievous construction, in which oriental-spicy classicism is intermingled with the sparkling freshness of citrus fruits and leaves. *OH LA LA* is a dazzling composition of fruity-floral-fresh notes on a theme of sandalwood, vanilla, and spice.
Bottle Design: Loris Azzaro and Serge Mansau have created an extraordinary baroque bottle in which the art of decoration meets the modernity of a new way of being. The dome-bottle, with facets of diamond-like purity, is set majestically on a crystalline pedestal, sculpted with spiraling volutes.
Package Design: Matte red and gold open the ball as if it were a cordial invitation to luxury and passion. Inside the dazzling box, a deep, bewitching midnight blue reveals the secret of the bottle, like a clear glass goblet filled with liquid gold.
Pictured Size: .10oz.
Dimensions: 2-1/2" h x 1" w
CPG:$10.00

Other Azzaro Fragrances

Azzaro®
Launch Date: 1970
Fragrance Type: Parfum:
Fruity, floral, and mossy.

Fun Facts
on Emperor Theodosius
Under the rule of Emperor Theodosius, known for his eccentric, manic love of scents, prisoners were required to be sprayed with rose water.

BAGHDAD

Fragrance of Baghdad®
Launch Date: Undetermined
Pictured Size: .25oz.
Dimensions: 1-3/4" h x 3/4" w
CPG: $30.00

BALENCIAGA
Cristobal Balenciaga
Balenciaga, Inc.

Eau de Balenciaga Lavande®
Launch Date: 1973
Fragrance Type: Eau de Toilette: Lavender
Pictured Size: .07oz.
Dimensions: 1-1/4" h x 3/4" w
CPG: $4.00

le dix®
Launch Date: 1947
Fragrance Type: Perfume: A perfume for all times, combining with ease the decades of this century. Today, *"LE DIX"* by BALENCIAGA is still a great contemporary classic. It was the *first* perfume created by Cristobal BALENCIAGA, named after the address of the famous couturier 10 Avenue George V. *"LE DIX"* evokes softness and beauty, romanticism and balance. It has the scent of a delicate, rare flower, and incarnates a woman at once refined and mysterious, irresistible and eternal. Under its flowery, tender and refined mantle, she will have the tranquil beauty of harmony, and natural charm and grace. Head notes of bergamot and lemon with middle notes of rose, ylang-ylang and lily-of-the-valley. Bottom notes are iris, sandalwood, vetiver, musk and vanilla.
Bottle Design: Fluted crystal bottle.
Package Design: Elegant white box with the signature black bow.
Pictured Size: .10oz.
Dimensions: 1-3/4" h x 3/4" w
CPG: $5.00

Fun Facts
on Cristobal Balenciaga
Cristobal Balenciaga's fashions are a permanent part of the collection at the Costume Institute of the Metropolitan Museum of Art in New York.

Michelle®
Launch Date: 1979
Fragrance Type: Perfume: Leafy greens, fruity notes, and a hint of floral create the top notes in this sensual fragrance. Exotic floral middle notes enhance the sweet, woody, and powdery base notes.
Bottle Design: Dramatic black, red, and gold stripes.
Package Design: Dramatic black, red, and gold stripes.
Pictured Size: .16oz.
Dimensions: 1-3/4" h x 1-1/2" w
CPG: $5.00

Cialenga®
Launch Date: 1973
Fragrance Type: Parfum: Top notes of citrus oils and fruity notes are blended with floral, woody, and powdery notes.
Pictured Size: .125oz.
Dimensions: 1-1/4" h x 1-1/8" w
CPG: $6.00

Rumba®
Launch Date: April, 1988
Fragrance Type: Eau de Toilette: Oriental-Florals
Pictured Size: .13oz.
Dimensions: 2" h x 1-1/8" w
CPG: $8.00

Talisman®
Launch Date: 1995

Fragrance Type: Perfume: A remembrance of time immemorial, *Talisman* also symbolizes the ties between past and present with a fragrance both eternal and resolutely modern. The *Talisman* fragrance associates the feminine sensuousness of chypre with the classicism of pungent floral scents, in their deliciously fruity under notes. The top notes are a fleeting impression of floral-fruit harmonies (violet leaf) with unique scents of litchi, dried fruits and osmanthus, accented by a hint of rum and Davana. The warm middle notes are derived from a compound of rose, jasmine, hyacinth, lily-of-the-valley, freesia, and cyclamen, revealing the full splendor and subtlety of a rich woody harmony of vibrant patchouli and sensuous sandalwood. The bottom notes linger in a powdery, shimmering symphony, mellowed by citrus in counterpoint to vanilla, underscored by rich absolute of beeswax.

Bottle Design: Every bottle of fragrance is a *Talisman*, incarnating in its form as in its content the most powerful magic—that of seduction. *Talisman* is sensuous forms, bold dissymmetry, and classic elegance. A technical feat: the base of the bottle, enlaced like the neck (by the Fashion-designer's thread), embraces the swelling forms of the asymmetrical glass-drop bottle. The translucent mauve stopper evokes the promise of an opening blossom, the elegantly fluid grace of an evening gown.

Package Design: Born under the sun sign of Cristobal BALENCIAGA, the brilliant yellow TALISMAN is punctuated by a gather held by three threads the gold of the double B logo.

Pictured Size: Photo Courtesy of Fragrance Marketing Group

Other Balenciaga Fragrances

Balenciaga® Pour Homme
Launch Date: October, 1990

Fragrance Type: Eau de Toilette: The success of *HO HANG* transcended fashion and maintained a faithful following. But a masculine presence which could thrust the BALENCIAGA Spirit into the world of Contemporary Man was missing. That is how *BALENCIAGA POUR HOMME* was born. *BALENCIAGA POUR HOMME* glorifies fantasy in a warm, sensual atmosphere. Its fragrance is finely tuned to that round, warm, enchanting world conducive to unrestricted sensations and imagination. It evokes the perfect refinement of former

34

Mediterranean civilizations—the Balenciaga Spirit. Ingredients are: Cinnamon from China and Ceylon, pepper, coriander, cardamom, thyme, laurel, galbanum, Italian bergamot, cyprenum vitae, patchouli, sandalwood, Yugoslavia moss, bourbon vanilla, honey, labdanum, and musk.

Ho Hang®
Launch Date: 1971
Fragrance Type: Eau de Toilette: *HO HANG* was BALENCIAGA's first perfume for men. Specially designed to be shared joyfully, *HO HANG* is the perfume of harmony, the balance between the masculine and the feminine. Fresh and tasteful, *HO HANG* is a distinguished eau de toilette which reigns without being overbearing, and is noticeable yet not overwhelming. It offers a highly original presence with such woody essences as cedar and vetiver, and spicy scents of sandalwood, coriander, musk, and more. Venus and Apollo could not have resisted its light charm, its aerial freshness, and its subtle, disarming power.

Prélude®
Launch Date: 1982
Fragrance Type: Perfume: Spicy notes highlight the top notes while florals and spice define the middle notes. Base notes are balsamic, sweet, and ambered.

Quadrille®
Launch Date: 1955 (1956 U.S.A.)
Fragrance Type: Parfum: Light, fresh, and fruity top notes blended with classic floral middle notes and woody, mossy base notes.

BARYSHNIKOV
Mikhail Baryshnikov
Richard Barrie Fragrances, Inc.

Baryshnikov® Pour Homme
Launch Date: March, 1991
Fragrance Type: Eau de Toilette: The fragrance draws its classic appeal from an artful blend of precious sandalwood, masculine amber and sensual patchouli. A reckless side is revealed in

the unusual blend of spice top notes that range from French coriander and sage oil to basil.

Bottle Design: Working with Pierre Dinand, Baryshnikov envisioned a bottle whose shape made a strong, but subtle impression and whose dark onyx exterior bespeaks of the mystery of modern man. The cool curves of the flacon invite the senses to touch and experience the fragrance. The bottle is topped by a domed cap, whose translucent blue tone provides a striking visual contrast to the dark reflections of the bottle.

Package Design: Created by graphic designer, Georges Gotlib, the charcoal carton is simply adorned with the silver foiled Baryshnikov name and a graphic representation of the celestial blue dome which top the fragrance bottle. The combination of blue and black in the bottle and packaging echoes the design statement made with the *Misha* fragrance and represents a color combination that Baryshnikov has personally always found aesthetically powerful.

Pictured Size: .27oz.
Dimensions: 2-1/4" h x 1-3/4" w
CPG: $10.00

Baryshnikov® Pour Femme

Launch Date: March, 1995

Fragrance Type: Parfum: A white floral bouquet on a musky, woody drydown. The top notes are a vibrant and colorful combination of exotic fruity and "petal-like" floralcy. A velvety smooth array of night blooming florals inspired by a romantic bride's bouquet create the middle notes while the dry down is of warm woods and enticing captive musk that enhance the fragrant feminine allure.

Bottle Design: Same as *Baryshnikov Pour Homme* except in a clear bottle with a green cap.

Package Design: Cream colored carton adorned with the Baryshnikov celestial dome. The dome area is a combination of teal, light blue and bronze.

Pictured Size: .27oz.
Dimensions: 1-1/4" h x 1-3/4" w
CPG: $20.00

Fun Facts
on Mikhail Baryshnikov
"Leaving Russia in 1974, Baryshnikov has been a featured dancer (ballet), as well as, his screen presence in feature films such as "White Night" and "Turning Point," for which he was nominated for an Academy Award.

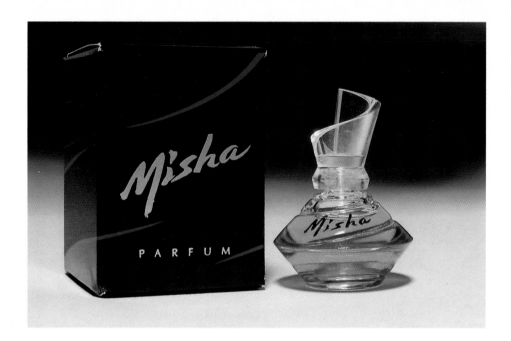

Misha®
Launch Date: 1989
Fragrance Type: Parfum
Pictured Size: .125oz.
Dimensions: 1-1/8" h x 1-3/4" w
CPG: $20.00

Fun Facts
First Sense
The sense of smell is located in the most primitive area of the brain
known as the limbic system. Because of its location, our sense
of smell matures before any of our other senses.

BENETTON
Benetton Cosmetics Corporation

Fun Facts
on Benetton
"Benetton Cosmetics was one of the first cosmetics companies to ban animal testing
and for nearly six years has worked toward changing the way the cosmetics
industry traditionally has treated animals. In 1990 PETA (People for
the Ethical Treatment of Animals) conferred its Humanitarian Award
to Benetton Cosmetics for their commitment to manufacturing high
quality products without harming animals," says Ms. Newkirk.
PETA

Colors De Benetton® for Women
Launch Date: 1986

Fragrance Type: Eau de Toilette: Semi-Oriental. *Colors De Benetton for Women* is fresh, bright and playful. It's a celebration of color. Top notes include coriander, passion fruit, and marigold oil blended with heart notes of jasmine, rose, and peach extract. Base notes include oak moss, patchouli, and vanilla.

Bottle Design: The fragrance bottle, which still features the pentagonal shape and *Colors* scripted logo, is manufactured in deep, green translucent glass.

Package Design: In 1993 the packaging of *Colors De Benetton* was redesigned to offer a new image that is more in tune with the 1990s. The beautiful, softer new outer packaging, which is a celebration of the natural elements of the world, emphasizes neutral colors and an uncoated finish. The cartons are environmentally friendly, made of recycled paper, and use vegetable-based inks.

Pictured Size: .13oz.

Dimensions: 2" h x 3/4" w

CPG: $9.00

Colors De Benetton® for Men
Launch Date: 1988

Fragrance Type: Eau de Toilette: Herbal-Oriental. A clean, crisp fragrance full of universal appeal. Like the women's, it combines ingredients from all over the world for a uniquely diverse scent. Top notes of citrus, lime, and mandarin flow into heart notes of sandalwood, cedarwood, and patchouli. Base notes are oakmoss, amber, and cedarmoss.

Bottle Design: The fragrance bottle, which still feature the pentagonal shape and *Colors* scripted logo, is manufactured in cobalt blue glass.

Package Design: In 1993 the packaging of *Colors De Benetton* was redesigned to offer a new image that is more in tune with the 1990s. The beautiful, softer new outer packaging, which is a celebration of the natural elements of the world, will emphasize neutral colors and an uncoated finish. The cartons are environmentally friendly, made of recycled paper, and use vegetable-based inks.

Pictured Size: .13oz.

Dimensions: 2" h x 3/4" w

CPG: $7.00

Origins of Colors
Russia
Morocco
Italy
Caribbean
Egypt
France
Bulgaria
Comores Islands
United States
Yugoslavia
China
Madagascar
Ethiopia
Brazil

United Colors of Benetton Tribù®
"REAL BEAUTY FOR REAL PEOPLE"
Launch Date: Fall, 1993
Fragrance Type: Parfum: Blending exotic flowers, fruits, plants, and woods that have long been mainstays of tribal health and beauty. *Tribù is made from all-natural or nature-identical elements. The line is made without animal by-products and is non-animal tested.*
Bottle Design: Tamotsu Yagi, world renowned graphic designer, created all visual elements of the *Tribu* line. The spectacular amber and rich red bottle is a completely new creation which merges modern technology with colors and designs found in nature. The fragrance bottle consists of a glass bottle encased in surlyn, an exotic, tactile plastic that diffuses light. The graceful, elongated shape manages to incorporate both angles and curves. *The extraordinary bottle is part of the permanent collection of the San Francisco Museum of Modern Art's Architecture and Design collection.*
Package Design: The outer packaging is a continuation of Tamotsu Yagi's artistic integrity. All of the cartons are made of recycled paper, and in a highly artistic, yet simple fashion, take their inspiration from the natural notes and centerures found in nature.
Pictured Size: .13oz.
Dimensions: 2-3/4" h x 1" w
CPG: $15.00

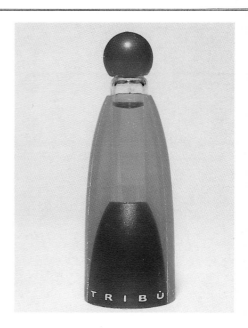

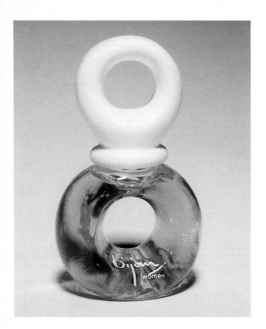

BIJAN
Bijan Fragrances, Inc.

Bijan® Perfume for Women
Launch Date: 1987
Fragrance Type: Eau de Parfum: Floriental—
Bijan Perfume for Women is a rare creation
capturing the elegance of a time-honored era and
the brilliance of a contemporary masterpiece. The
top note of exotic ylang-ylang, narcisse, and orange
flower harmonizes with the enduring heart notes
of Persian jasmine, muguet, and precious rose
bulgare. This mysterious blend evolves into a
Floriental composition. delicately enhanced by
sultry patchouli, Moroccan oakmoss, and soothing
sandalwood.
Bottle Design: by Bijan
Package Design: by Bijan & Daniela Pakzad.
Pictured Size: .25oz.
Dimensions: 2-3/4" h x 1-1/2" w
CPG: $15.00

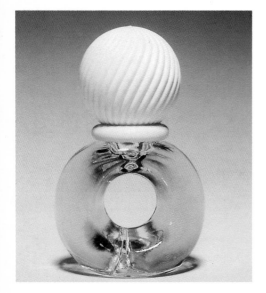

Bijan® Fragrance for Men
"For men...of substance!"
Launch Date: 1987
Fragrance Type: Eau de Toilette: First men's
scent. Contemporary and discerning characterize
two incisive qualities of the forever-compelling
Bijan Man. Exotic citrus harmonizes with the
freshness of Italian bergamot to create a very
distinct first impression while rosemary blends
with lavender bringing uplifting qualities. Spicy
nutmeg and vetiver intermingle with exotic
patchouli and rare sandalwood to introduce a
mysterious woody aura. Strong masculine
sophistication is captured in musk, amber, and
oakmoss to reveal the final and lasting characteristic.
Bottle Design: by Bijan
Package Design: by Bijan & Daniela Pakzad.
Pictured Size: .25oz.
Dimensions: 2-3/4" h x 1-1/2" w
CPG: $15.00

Fun Facts
on Bijan
"Bijan says: "The world said to conform, the world said settle for less,
the world said compromise and no one will
know...so I made my own world!"
Bijan

Bijan

Bijan's DNA® Perfume for Women

"It's the reason you have your father's eyes, your mother's smile and...Bijan's perfume!"

Launch Date: 1993

Fragrance Type: Eau de Parfum: Floramber Naturelle: Stirred and stimulated by the emotions of the wearer, the 193 rare and precious ingredients blend in harmony to create this captivating fragrance—romantic, soft, yet seductive and spirited—mysterious as the woman herself. *Bijan's DNA* Perfume for Women gracefully introduces itself with a hypnotic intensity of rosewood for a fresh, mellow "burst," minty geranium for strength, ylang-ylang for richness, and bergamot for zest and originality. As the scent blossoms, a beautiful feminine bouquet of jasmine, muguet, and white tuberose combine with spicy clove and fruity osmanthus for sparkle and warmth, creating a spiritual sensuality that is cheerfully confident and frankly feminine. The fragrance evolves into a rich, earthy essence with ancient, haunting myrrh offering mystery and tenacity as oakmoss lends a green and refreshing tone. Sandalwood and vetiver instill deep, inviting aspects, while vanilla and benzoin lace the composition with a soft, amber undertone...creating a new fragrance family, ***Floramber Naturelle***, the first classification of its kind dedicated to this distinctive fragrance.

Bottle Design: Presented in a distinctive flacon formed by three embracing strands intertwined as one.

Package Design: by Bijan & Daniela Pakzad.

Pictured Size: .16oz.

Dimensions: 2-1/8" h x 3/4" w

CPG: $12.50

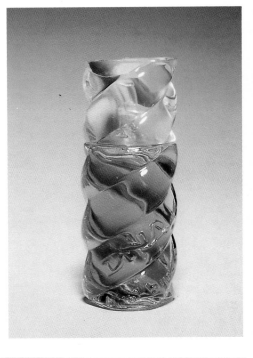

DNA.
P E R F U M E ®

by *Bijan*®

Bijan's DNA® for Men
Launch Date: 1993
Fragrance Type: Eau de Toilette: Spirited Aromatic Woods: Created by Bijan. Aromatic woods entice fresh citrus notes to deliver an energizing burst of herbs and rich spices...creating a unique natural signature. The vitality and lasting intrigue of *Bijan's DNA for Men* is attributed to its centerural composition...a *Spirited Aromatic Woods* fragrance. Top notes—the energy of luscious Spanish mandarin harmonizes with the freshness of Italian bergamot to create a very distinct first impression. Rosemary endures with clove and juniper berry, bringing stimulating vitality. Middle notes—seductive jasmine is empowered with the uplifting quality of lavender while soothing sandalwood intermingles with earthy cedar and exotic patchouli to introduce a regenerating aura. Dry down notes—a masculine sophistication is captured in the resonance of vanilla, tenacious amber, and warm traces of oakmoss to reveal an enduring gentle strength.
Bottle Design: Bijan's *DNA* Eau de Toilette for Men is presented in a distinctive cobalt blue flacon formed by three embracing strands intertwined as one.
Package Design: by Bijan & Daniela Pakzad.
Pictured Size: .16oz.
Dimensions: 2-1/8" h x 3/4" w
CPG: $12.50

BILL BLASS
Revlon, Inc.

Bill Blass®
Launch Date: 1978
Fragrance Type: Perfume: Fruity and green top notes. Exotic florals blend with sensual, powdery base notes.
Pictured Size: .125oz.
Dimensions: 1-1/2" h x 1" w
CPG: $5.00

Basic Black®
Launch Date: 1990
Fragrance Type: Perfume: Chypre-Floral.
Pictured Size: .125oz.
Dimensions: 1-1/2" h x 1" w
CPG: $5.00

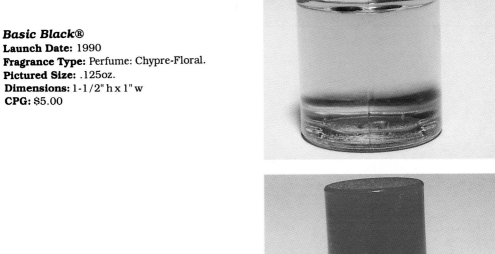

Hot®
Launch Date: 1990
Fragrance Type: Perfume: Fruity-Floral.
Pictured Size: .125oz.
Dimensions: 1-1/2" h x 1" w
CPG: $5.00

Nude®
Launch Date: 1990
Fragrance Type: Perfume: Floral
Pictured Size: .125oz.
Dimensions: 1-1/2" h x 1" w
CPG: $5.00

43

BOB MACKIE
Riviera Concepts, Inc.

M odern
A ccomplished
C onfident
K nowing
I ntouch
E xciting

Mackie, Bob Mackie®

Launch Date: February, 1991

Fragrance Type: Perfume: *Mackie* is a modern, rich, floral oriental (floriental) bouquet. Witty, fruity top notes melt into a rich white floral body. Sensuous oriental notes add depth and tenacity.

Bottle Design: Bob Mackie and famed French bottle designer, Pierre Dinand, have captured the glamour and glitz of *Mackie* in a bottle and box. The classic multi-faceted crystalline bottle and striking stopper reflect Mackie's love of crystal. A touch of glamour is added to the perfume with the black and gold tassel.

Package Design: Mackie's design elements are evident in the outer packaging—classic black, glamorous gold, and a dazzling array of five stunning colors. The Mackie colors: *BLACK*, classic, mystical, magical; *GOLD*, glamorous, brilliant; *MAGENTA*, sensual, feminine; *ORANGE*, radiant, vibrant, fun; *GREEN*, harmonizing, cool, *CHARTREUSE*, modern, bright; *RED*, intense, stimulating, sexy.

Pictured Size: .17oz. (Deluxe Miniature Size)
Dimensions: 2-1/2" h x 1" w
CPG: $15.00

M asculine
A dventurous
C harismatic
K een
I ntriguing
E nergetic

Mackie® for Men

Launch Date: September, 1992

Fragrance Type: Eau de Toilette: *Mackie For Men* is a modern, distinctive scent with a subtle persistence. Uniquely masculine, modern, and refined. A harmonious blend of fresh citrus with warm woody under notes, and a base of subtle musk and amber notes. The Mackie man is exciting.

44

Bottle Design: Modern, intriguing, and masculine describe the design concept of the *Mackie for Men* bottle and box. The commitment to style and quality is evident as we combine the talent of Bob Mackie and famed French bottle designer, Pierre Dinand. *Mackie for Men* is a sharply defined, angular, faceted flask. The design inspiration originated from the multi-faceted glass stopper on the women's fragrance bottle. The bottle is an extended version of this stopper. Sophisticated in its simplicity, the square set silver and black top caps the classic shape.

Package Design: Mackie's design elements are evident as Mackie for Men is the natural complement to his feminine fragrance. An outstanding array of colors offset the prism on the masculine gun metal background. The Mackie colors: *GUN METAL*, strong, distinguished; *BURGUNDY*, stimulating, sexy; *BLACK*, classic, masculine; *OCHRE*, unique, outstanding; *TEAL*, intriguing, cool, *OLIVE*, adventurous, sporty; *COPPER*, vibrant, fun.

Pictured Size: .20oz. (Deluxe Miniature Size)
Dimensions: 2-1/2"h x 1" w
CPG: $12.00

BORGHESE
Princess Marcella Borghese

Il Bacio®
Launch Date: 1993
Fragrance Type: Parfum: Floral
Pictured Size: .125oz.
Dimensions: 2 " x 1-1/4" w
CPG: $12.50

Other Borghese Fragrances

Andiamo®
Launch Date: 1970

Di Borghese®
Launch Date: 1978

Ecco®
Launch Date: 1960

Fiamma®
Launch Date: 1965

Boss
Hugo Boss

Boss®
Launch Date: 1985
Fragrance Type: Eau de Toilette: Fougère
Pictured Size: .17oz.
Dimensions: 2" h x 1-1/8" w
CPG: $7.00

Other Hugo Boss Fragrances

Boss Spirit®
Launch Date: 1989
Fragrance Type: Eau de Toilette: Chypre-Leathery.

Boss Sport®
Launch Date: 1987
Fragrance Type: Eau de Toilette: Fougère: Woody and ambered.
Pictured Size: .17oz.
Dimensions: 2" h x 1-1/8" w
CPG: $7.00

Hugo®
Launch Date: Fall, 1995
Fragrance Type: Top notes are green apple, pine needles, and spearmint. Middle notes are spicy and floral with base notes that are woody and leathery.
Bottle Design: Canteen style flask with a silver screw-on cap and canvas green strap.

Boucheron
Louis Boucheron
Boucheron Corp. Parfums

Boucheron Classic®
Launch Date: 1988
Fragrance Type: Eau de Parfum: Semi-oriental florals.
Pictured Size: .17oz.
Dimensions: 1-3/4" h x 1-1/4" w
CPG: $13.00

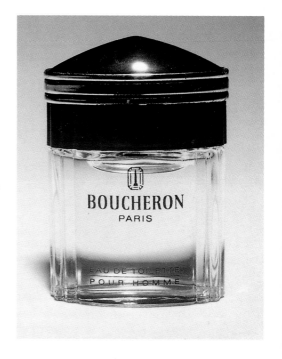

Boucheron® Pour Homme
Launch Date: 1991
Fragrance Type: Eau de Toilette: Fresh, woody notes.
Pictured Size: .20oz.
Dimensions: 1-3/4" h x 1-1/4" w
CPG: $8.00

Jaipur de Boucheron®
Launch Date: 1994
Fragrance Type: Eau de Parfum: Fruity, floral notes.
Pictured Size: .17oz.
Dimensions: 1-3/4" h x 1-1/2" w
CPG: $15.00

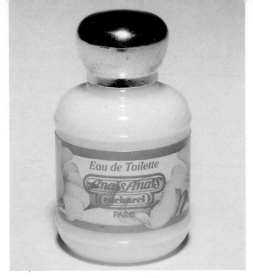

CACHAREL
Jean Bouquet Cacharel Parfums

Anaïs Anaïs®
Launch Date: 1978
Fragrance Type: Eau de Parfum: Fresh, floral notes mingled with woody, mossy base notes.
Bottle Design: Milk colored bottle with crowned silver top and signature pastel floral motif label.
Package Design: Cacharel's signature pastel floral motif.
Pictured Size: .23oz.
Dimensions: 1-3/4" h x 1" w
CPG: $9.00

Cacharel® Pour Homme
Launch Date: 1981
Fragrance Type: Eau de Toilette: Fougère
Bottle Design: Glass flask with rounded lines.
Pictured Size: .25oz.
Dimensions: 2-1/8" h x 1-1/8" w
CPG: $7.00

Lou Lou®
Launch Date: 1987
Fragrance Type: Eau de Parfum: Oriental
Pictured Size: .17oz.
Dimensions: 2-1/8" h x 1-1/2" w
CPG: $8.00

Other Cacharel Fragrances

Eden®
Launch Date: 1994

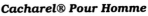

CAESARS
Caesars World Merchandising, Inc.

Caesars Woman®
Launch Date: 1987
Fragrance Type: Extravagant Perfume: A floral, spicy bouquet rich in Rose d'Orient, Egyptian jasmine, and orange flower, set against a background of exotic oils such as Tibetan musk, patchouli, and sandalwood such as were known in the days of Caesar.
Bottle Design: Presented in an exclusively designed "Lalique"-type crystal bottle, manufactured by hand in France.
Pictured Size: .125oz.
Dimensions: 1-3/8" h x 1-3/8" w
CPG: $8.00

Other Caesars Fragrances

Caesars Man®
"Wear it and conquer"
Launch Date: December, 1987
Fragrance Type: Legendary Cologne: A totally masculine scent, designed to capture the excitement of all that is the pleasure of Caesars Palace— the sporting life, the excess, the pleasures enjoyed by men of power—always in control of his destiny. This fragrance is presented as a signature of Caesar the Conqueror, and is not for the faint of heart. An effusive combination of herbaceous, lavender and citrus notes, it is balanced with warm, woody, and mossy under notes.

Ferentina®
"Indulge in the myth."—Ferentina; the goddess of woods and springs.
Launch Date: 1994

Palace Reserve®
Launch Date: 1988

Fun Facts
on Caesars World Merchandising
Caesars World Merchandising Inc., brings to life the regal grandeur of Ancient Rome. We support Athletes & Entertainers for Kids in their work to make the life of a less fortunate child rich with possibilities.
Deborah Christopher, President/CEO, Caesars World Merchandising, Inc.

CALVIN KLEIN
Calvin Klein Cosmetics

CK ONE™
Launch Date: Fall, 1994
Fragrance Type: Eau de Toilette: Bright and effervescent, the top notes are a combination of bergamot, cardamom, fresh pineapple, and papaya. The middle notes contain the highest quality of hedione high cis, (a special formulation derived from Jasmine), an aromatic that heightens and contributes to the lasting fluidity of the bouquet. Also includes violet, rose, and nutmeg. Two new musks combined with amber create a sensuous drydown completing the effect of fullness and warmth. The CK ONE™ fragrance is a balance between brightness and sensuality.
Bottle Design: The design of CK ONE™ bottle is naturally appealing to both men and women. CK ONE™ products are packaged in glass and aluminum containers which can be recycled (where programs and facilities exist). The sizes of CK ONE™ products are large and generous, encouraging liberal application resulting in a veil of lingering scent, one that invites closeness and intimacy.
Package Design: The CK ONE ™ collection reduces packaging to the essentials, avoiding the opulent outer packaging of most cosmetic products. The flasks of CK ONE™ eau de toilette are protected in shipping and handling by cartons made of 100% recycled cardboard, everything else is unadorned.
Pictured Size: .5oz.
Dimensions: 2-3/4" h x 1-1/2" w
CPG: $10.00

ESCAPE®
Launch Date: Fall, 1991
Fragrance Type: Parfum: Fresh, fruity, floral bouquet blended with a heart of exotic spices and a woody sensuous background. This fragrance suggests a philosophy of living life intensely, so that every moment counts.
Bottle Design: Collaborated with Pierre Dinand. Faceted clear crystal bottle topped with a silver-toned top inspired by an antique perfume bottle in Kelly Klein's personal collection.
Package Design: Parchment-inspired outer package in ivory modeled after a 19th century travel case.
Pictured Size: .13oz.
Dimensions: 1" h x 3/4" w
CPG: $12.50 (Beauty Sampler Only)

ESCAPE® *for men*

Launch Date: Fall, 1993

Fragrance Type: Eau de Toilette: *ESCAPE®* for men fragrance is a fresh, clean scent of birch leaf. It is so unique it has a category of its own: cool, woody, fresh. "*ESCAPE®* for men fragrance reflects the need every man has to make his life an adventure." —Calvin Klein

Bottle Design: Inspired from an antique silver shave brush holder in Klein's own collection. Calvin Klein collaborated once again with re-nowned Pierre Dinand to design the modern, dramatic frosted glass cylinder topped with a silver-toned cap.

Package Design: Parchment-inspired outer package in ivory modeled after a 19th century travel case.

Pictured Size: .5oz.

Dimensions: 2-3/4" h x 1" w

CPG: $8.00 (Beauty Sampler Only)

ETERNITY®

Launch Date: Spring, 1988

Fragrance Type: Parfum: Contemporary version of the classic floral scent. *ETERNITY®* fragrance was inspired when Calvin Klein gave to his wife, Kelly, a beautiful antique wedding ring from the collection of the Duchess of Windsor inscribed with one word, "eternity." About *ETERNITY®* Calvin Klein says, "Romance with commitment. That's what today's woman wants."

Bottle Design: Collaborated with Pierre Dinand. Elegantly dimensioned geometric clear crystal bottle, cut with beveled edges and capped with a silver top.

Package Design: White packaging with gray detailing.

Pictured Size: .13oz.

Dimensions: 1-3/4" h x 1" w

CPG: $12.50 (Beauty Sampler Only)

ETERNITY® for men
Launch Date: Fall, 1989
Fragrance Type: Eau de Toilette: A fresh, modern scent for today's man: sensitive yet masculine. The essence of the fragrance comes from crisp, clean, fresh, refined yet strong scents that are distinctive. Top notes include mandarin, lavender, and rain fresh greens. The heart of this fragrance blends jasmine, basil, geranium, orange flower, tarragon, and sage. Bottom notes are sandalwood, vetiver, rosewood, and amber.
Bottle Design: Calvin Klein collaborated with celebrated designer Pierre Dinand to interpret a masculine version of the ETERNITY® fragrance bottle design (heavy glass with rounded shoulders) incorporating silver and crystal to represent the timeless ideal of romance with commitment.
Package Design: Gray packaging with white detailing.
Pictured Size: .5oz.
Dimensions: 2-1/2" h x 1-3/8" w
CPG: $8.00 (Beauty Sampler Only)

Fun Facts
Obsession®
"Bottle design inspired from Calvin Klein's collection of Indian prayer stones."
Calvin Klein Cosmetics

OBSESSION®
Launch Date: Spring, 1985
Fragrance Type: Parfum: An intoxicating blend of florals and spices with an earthy, warm base creating an intensely feminine and lasting scent. About OBSESSION® Calvin Klein says, "I imagined the mystique of a woman who allows herself to experience a romantic obsession—and one who invites a man to do the same."
Bottle Design: Collaborated with Pierre Dinand. Heavy, rounded clear bottle with a brown mock tortoise top.
Package Design: Ivory box with indigo detailing.
Pictured Size: .12oz.
Dimensions: 1" h x 1-1/2" w
CPG: $12.50 (Beauty Sampler Only)

OBSESSION® *for men*

Launch Date: Fall, 1986

Fragrance Type: Eau de Toilette: Provocative, fiery, and masculine, the top notes are fruity and mingle with middle notes that are spicy while base notes are ambered, musky and woody. "Men have always been driven by their passions—whether in work or romance, and I wanted to create a scent that would exude that determination and fire." — Calvin Klein. The pure essence of masculinity. A compelling blend of botanics, spices and rare woods creating a potent, powerful, and intensely provocative scent.

Bottle Design: Collaborated with Pierre Dinand. Flask-like clear bottle with a mock tortoise stopper.

Package Design: Ivory box with indigo detailing.

Pictured Size: .5oz.

Dimensions: 2-3/4" h x 1-3/4" w

CPG: $8.00 (Beauty Sampler Only)

CAPUCCI
Roberto Capucci
Parfums Capucci, Paris

Capucci de Capucci®

Launch Date: 1987

Fragrance Type: Perfume

Bottle Design: Inspired by a Roberto Capucci gown, Pierre Dinand designed the bottle in the "billowing gown" style with the faceted and frosted glass representing the effect of material.

Package Design: Shocking pink and turquoise.

Pictured Size: .17oz.

Dimensions: 1-1/2" h x 1-3/4" w

CPG: $9.00

Graffiti®

Launch Date: 1963

Fragrance Type: Perfume: Fresh, green, notes and fresh florals are blended with mossy, powdery base notes.

Pictured Size: .06oz.

Dimensions: 1-1/2" h x 3/4" w

CPG: $5.00

Yendi®
Launch Date: 1974
Fragrance Type: Perfume: Fruity top notes with heart notes of elegant florals and sensual, feminine, powdery base notes.
Pictured Size: .17oz.
Dimensions: 2" h x 1-3/8" w
CPG: $5.00

Other Capucci Fragrances

Filly®
Launch Date: 1983

CARA NOME
Dist. by Langlois, Inc.

Cara Nome®
Launch Date: c. 1918
Pictured Size: .125oz.
Dimensions: 2-1/8" h x 3/4" w
CPG: $12.00

tish tish®
Launch Date: 1900s
Fragrance Type: Perfume
Pictured Size: .125oz.
Dimensions: 2" h x 3/4" w
CPG: $15.00

CAROLINA HERRERA
Carolina Herrera Perfumes

Carolina Herrera®
Launch Date: 1988
Fragrance Type: Eau de Parfum: Floral
Pictured Size: .13oz.
Dimensions: 2" h x 1-1/8" w
CPG: $10.00

Herrera® for Men
Launch Date: 1991
Fragrance Type: Eau de Toilette: Fougère
Pictured Size: .20oz.
Dimensions: 2-3/8" h x 1" w
CPG: $9.00

Other Carolina Herrera Fragrances

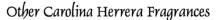

Flore®
Launch Date: September, 1994
Fragrance Type: Parfum: Light florals of iris, lily
of the valley, and jasmine.
Bottle Design: Designer Andre Ricard. The cap is
a floral bouquet; the body acts as a pedestal for
the floral bouquet cap.
Package Design: Famous Herrera signature polka
dot fashion with her logo set on a coral red
background.

CARON
Ernest Daltroff Parfums Caron Paris

Fleurs de Rocaille®
Launch Date: 1934
Fragrance Type: Eau de Toilette: Fresh floral top notes blended with spicy floral notes.
Pictured Size: .07oz.
Dimensions: 1-1/4" h x 1" w
CPG: $6.00

Fleurs de Rocaille®
Launch Date: 1934
Fragrance Type: Eau de Toilette: Fresh floral top notes blended with spicy, floral notes.
Pictured Size: .10oz.
Dimensions: 1-1/2" h x 1" w
CPG: $10.00

Infini®
Launch Date: 1970
Fragrance Type: Parfum: Fruity, green top notes blended with classic, elegant floral heart notes. Woody, powdery, and feminine notes define the base notes.
Pictured Size: .30oz.
Dimensions: 2-1/8" h x 1-3/4" w
CPG: $25.00

Le Ze Homme®
Launch Date: 1985
Fragrance Type: Fougère
Pictured Size: .34oz.
Dimensions: 2" h x 1-3/4" w
CPG: $5.00

Other Caron Fragrances

Adastra®
Launch Date: 1936
Fragrance Type: Floral

Alpona®
Launch Date: 1939
Fragrance Type: Floral and woody notes.

Bellodgia®
Launch Date: 1927
Fragrance Type: Eau de Toilette: Spicy top notes enhance the floral middle notes. Base notes are sweet and powdery.

Eau de Caron®
Launch Date: 1980
Fragrance Type: Woody, floral notes blended to perfection with citrusy notes.

En Avion®
Launch Date: 1930
Fragrance Type: Spicy, floral, musky notes.

French Cancan®
Launch Date: 1936
Fragrance Type: Woody-Floral notes.

L'Infini®
Launch Date: 1912

La Fete de Roses®
Launch Date: 1936
Fragrance Type: Floral and musk notes.

Le Muguet de Bonheur®
Launch Date: 1952
Fragrance Type: Simple floral notes.

Narcisse Noir®
Launch Date: 1911
Fragrance Type: Citrus and flowery top notes blend elegantly into dry floral middle notes. Base notes are soft and sensual florals.

N'Aimez Que Moi®
Launch Date: 1916

Nocturnes®
Launch Date: 1981
Fragrance Type: Leafy greens and fruity notes are used to create top notes. Middle notes are floral and blend into sweet, woody base notes.

Nuit de Noel®
Launch Date: 1922

Or et Noir®
Launch Date: 1949
Fragrance Type: Eastern rose, warm and spicy notes are the base of this floral composition.

Pois de Senteur de chez moi®
Launch Date: 1927
Fragrance Type: Florals

Poivre®
Launch Date: 1954
Fragrance Type: Floral and woody notes.

Sacre®
Launch Date: 1990

Tabac Blond®
Launch Date: 1919
Fragrance Type: Perfume: Top notes are spicy and citrusy. Middle notes are classic florals and blend into base notes of tobacco, leather, and powdery notes.

Voeu de Noel®
Launch Date: 1939
Fragrance Type: Floral bouquet of roses, lilac, and carnation. Originally named "ROSE DE NOEL".

Yatagan®
Launch Date: 1976

Voyage®
Launch Date: Undetermined

with pleasure®
Launch Date: 1949 & Reintroduced 1984
Fragrance Type: Florals such as jasmine, rose, and hyacinth.

CARTIER
Cartier

Panthère® de Cartier
Launch Date: 1988
Fragrance Type: Parfum: Floral
Pictured Size: .13oz.
Dimensions: 2-1/4" h x 1-3/4" w
CPG: $12.00

So Pretty® de Cartier
Launch Date: 1995
Fragrance Type: Eau de Parfum: Floral bouquet.
Pictured Size: .13oz.
Dimensions: 2-1/4" h x 3/4" w
CPG: $15.00 (Gift Set)

Other Cartier Fragrances

Must de Cartier®
Launch Date: 1981
Fragrance Type: Oriental: Spicy and ambered.

Must de Cartier 11®
Launch Date: 1981
Fragrance Type: Fougère

Panthère®
Launch Date: 1986
Fragrance Type: Oriental

Pasha de Cartier®
Launch Date: 1992
Fragrance Type: Fougère

Santos® de Cartier
Launch Date: 1981
Fragrance Type: Oriental: Spicy and ambered.

Santos® Eau de Sport P.H.
Launch Date: 1989
Fragrance Type: Oriental: Spicy and ambered.

CARVEN

Parfums Carven Paris

Ma Griffe®
Launch Date: 1946
Fragrance Type: Parfum: Signature fragrance.
This chypre fragrance begins with green the top notes. Green, woody, and floral notes create the middle notes and are blended with mossy, balsamic base notes.
Bottle Design: Repackaged in 1975 in a classically simple, neat, uncluttered line bottle topped with a gold stopper in the shape of the CARVEN "C".
Package Design: In its green and white stripe packaging, it embodies youth and "joie de vivre."(Joie de vivre: a carefree, joyful enjoyment of life).
Pictured Size: .17oz.
Dimensions: 2-1/8" h x 3/4" w
CPG: $7.00

> **Fun Facts**
> Ma Griffe®
> Means—My Signature

Vétiver®
Launch Date: 1957
Fragrance Type: Eau de Toilette: Light, yet with a certain sharpness, this masculine fragrance was born from the lemon of Grasse and green, warm, and woody base notes.
Bottle Design: Repackaged in 1975 in a classically simple, neat, uncluttered line bottle topped with a gold stopper in the shape of the CARVEN "C".
Package Design: In its green and white stripe packaging, it embodies youth and "joie de vivre."
Pictured Size: .17oz.
Dimensions: 2-1/8" h x 3/4" w
CPG: $9.00

Eau Vive®
Launch Date: 1966
Fragrance Type: The first eau de toilette not
derived from a perfume which opened the way for
many other "eaux fraîches."

Guirlandes®
Launch Date: 1982
Fragrance Type: Fruity top notes blend into
delicate floral middle notes. Base notes are sweet,
ambered, and powdery in this fresh, romantic, and
youthful fragrance.
Bottle Design: Lovingly packaged in a flowery
bottle, decorated with graduations of bright and
tender pinks.

Intrigue®
"...every promise has its secret."
Launch Date: 1986
Fragrance Type: Classic floral fragrance.

Madame de Carven®
**"To celebrate the "self-assured woman of our
times."**
Launch Date: 1979
Fragrance Type: Fresh, fruity top notes are
blended with exotic floral middle notes. Base notes
are warm, ambered, and woody.
Bottle Design: For the enhancement of these
warm, opulent scents Carven has created a
luxurious environment. The golden liquid

cascades within the myriad swirls of the bottle
topped by the unfurled tortoise-shell wings of the
stopper.
Package Design: The "coffrets" and the boxes
both express the richness of this creation in the
play of warm color graduations embellished in
gold.

Monsieur Carven®
Launch Date: 1978
Fragrance Type: Deliberately modern, this
fragrance is woody, warm, and spicy.
Bottle Design: Sober, square, and masculine.

Robe D'Un Soir®
Launch Date: 1947
Fragrance Type: Glamour and distinction gave
emphasis to the emergence of Woman's new
personality.

Variations®
Launch Date: 1971
Fragrance Type: Citrus and florals create the top
notes while green accords and florals are at the
heart. Base notes are mild florals, powdery, and
mossy.

Vetiver Dry®
Launch Date: 1988
Fragrance Type: Reemphasize the classic Vetiver
name.

OTHER CARVEN FRAGRANCES

Cassini
Oleg Cassini Cassini Parfums Ltd.

Cassini®
"A Love Affair That Never Ends"
Launch Date: March, 1990 (U.S.A.)
Fragrance Type: Eau de Parfum: Fruity, floral chypre with a floral heart blended together with rich bottom notes of amber and mousse de chene.
Bottle Design: Rounded, heavy clear glass bottle with amethyst snap-on top. Signature name is on front of bottle in gold tone color.
Package Design: Packaged in signature moire carton with gold embossing.
Pictured Size: .125oz.
Dimensions: 1-1/2" h x 1" w
CPG: $8.00

Cassini® *for Men*
"THE ART OF SEDUCTION"
Launch Date: Fall, 1994 (U.S.A.)
Fragrance Type: Eau de Toilette: Fresh, fruity, and woody notes create this sportive fragrance.
Bottle Design: Clear crystal enhanced by a sculpted silver plated collar (not on miniature size bottles) crowned by a sapphire blue snap-on cap. Signature name is on front of bottle in silver. *Cassini for Men* represents the extension of the women's thought.
Package Design: Reflects the shaded ombre notes of *Cassini*'s sapphire blue, accented by shafts of pure silver.
Pictured Size: .25oz.
Dimensions: 2-1/4" h x 1-1/4" w
CPG: $5.00

Fun Facts
on Oleg Cassini
"Oleg Cassini owns the smallest horse in the world at 19" tall: "Miracle Standing".
Cassini Parfums Ltd.

CHANEL
Chanel, Inc. Gabrielle Bonheur Chanel

Antaeus®
Launch Date: 1981
Fragrance Type: Pour Homme: Chypre-Leathery:
Warm, woody essence blended with herbal notes
and leathery base notes.
Bottle Design: Black glass flacon.
Package Design: Plum with black lacquer trim.
Pictured Size: .14oz.
Dimensions: 1-3/4" h x 3/4" w
CPG: $6.00

Chanel No. 5®
Launch Date: 1921
Fragrance Type: Parfum: Aldehydic: Citrusy top
notes blend with elegant floral middle notes. Base
notes are feminine, sweet, ambered, and powdery.
Pictured Size: .14oz.
Dimensions: 1-3/4" h x 1" w
CPG: $7.00

Fun Facts
On Chanel No. 5®
Five variations of this newly aldehyde fragrance were presented to Mademoiselle
Chanel to sample. Still bearing the number, she chose #5.

Coco®
Launch Date: 1984
Fragrance Type: Eau de Parfum: Oriental-Spicy.
Bottle Design: Clean lined glass bottle with simple black and white label and an emerald style faceted stopper.
Pictured Size: .14oz.
Dimensions: 1-3/4" h x 1" w
CPG: $7.00

Égoïste®
Launch Date: 1990
Fragrance Type: Eau de Toilette: Oriental-Spicy.
Pictured Size: .14oz.
Dimensions: 1-3/4" h x 3/4" w
CPG: $6.00

Other Chanel Fragrances

Bois de Îles®
Launch Date: 1926
Fragrance Type: Precious florals define both top and middle notes. Base notes are woody and sweet.

Chanel No. 19®
Launch Date: 1971
Fragrance Type: Green notes, elegant florals blended with woody, mossy notes.

Chanel No. 22®
Launch Date: 1922
Fragrance Type: Fruity top notes are blended with floral middle notes and sweet powdery base notes.

Cristalle®
Launch Date: 1993
Fragrance Type: Eau de Parfum: Chypre: Fresh, light, fruity, and floral notes blended with mossy base notes.

Cuir de Russie®
Launch Date: 1927
Fragrance Type: Floral, spices and green notes are blended with middle notes that are woody and floral. Base notes are balsamic and leathery.

Égoïste "Platinum"®
Launch Date: 1993
Fragrance Type: Fougère

Gardenia®
Launch Date: 1925
Fragrance Type: Floral

Pour Monsieur®
Launch Date: 1955
Fragrance Type: Oriental: Ambered and woody.

CHARLES JOURDAN
Parfums Charles Jourdan Paris

L'insolent®
Launch Date: 1986
Fragrance Type: Eau de Toilette: Floral: Fresh, fruity top notes blend into a heart of elegant light florals. Base notes are musky, woody, and mossy.
Pictured Size: .125oz.
Dimensions: 2-1/8" h x 1-3/4" w
CPG: $8.00

Other Jourdan Fragrances

Vôtre®
Launch Date: 1978
Fragrance Type: Top notes are fresh and green accords with radiant floral middle notes and light floral base notes.

CHARLES OF THE RITZ
Charles Jundt

Senchal®
Launch Date: 1981
Fragrance Type: Parfum: Floral and fruity accords create the top notes. Sweet, floral middle notes with base notes that are warm and woody.
Pictured Size: .125oz.
Dimensions: 2" h x 1" w
CPG: $5.00

Other Charles of the Ritz Fragrances

Charivari®
Launch Date: 1978
Fragrance Type: Fruity-Floral.

Fun Facts
Putting on the Ritz
Charles Jundt named his company Charles of the Ritz after opening his salon in the hotel Ritz-Carlton, New York City.

Charles of the Ritz®
Launch Date: 1977
Fragrance Type: Exotic florals and fruits.

Ritual®
Launch Date: 1945

Ritz®
Launch Date: 1972
Fragrance Type: Parfum: Peach and hyacinth help create the top notes. Jasmine, lily of the valley, carnation, and ylang-ylang contribute to a sweet, floral heart. Base notes are amber, musk, and mossy.

CHER

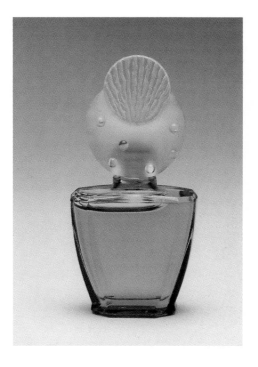

Cher Uninhibited®
Launch Date: 1988
Fragrance Type: Perfume: Floral
Pictured Size: .125oz.
Dimensions: 2-1/4" h x 1-1/8" w
CPG: $9.00

CHEVIGNON
Parfums Chevignon Paris

Chevignon® for Men
Launch Date: 1992 (1995 U.S.A.)
Fragrance Type: Eau de Toilette: *Youth* and *Freshness* spring forth from the top note, with the wild mint associated basil and bergamot. *Authentic* and *Preserved Nature*, in the green leaves which warm under the Tunisian sun: artemisia, oregano, and rosemary. *Promise of adventure and mystery*, wide open spaces, in the middle notes born of cedar and patchouli, enhanced by the resinous perfume of the Canadian pine. *Nostalgia*, like an autumn mist, the Virginia tobacco and Russian leather enrobe the bottom note, which is authentic and virile.
Pictured Size: Photo Courtesy of Fragrance Marketing Group
CPG: $9.00

CHOPARD

Căsmir®
Launch Date: 1991
Fragrance Type: Parfum: Fruity-Oriental.
Pictured Size: .10oz.
Dimensions: 1-1/4" h x 1" w
CPG: $7.00

CHRISTIAN DIOR
Christian Dior Perfumes, Inc.

Fun Facts
on Christian Dior
"Parfums Christian Dior was founded by Christian Dior and Serge
Heftler-Louiche in 1947 with its first perfume MISS DIOR®"
Christian Dior Perfumes

Diorissimo®
Launch Date: 1956
Fragrance Type: Perfume Classic: A lilting
fresh fragrance of tender romance, *DIORISSIMO*
is a whisper of spring. The blend of jasmine and
amaryllis mingles with delicate notes of lily of the
valley.
Pictured Size: .34oz.
Dimensions: 2-1/4" h x 1-1/4" w
CPG: $6.00

Fun Facts
Favorite Flower
"Lily of the Valley was Christian Dior's favorite flower."
Christian Dior Perfumes

Dune®
"UNITING NATURE AND WOMAN"
Launch Date: 1991 (1992 U.S.A.)

Fragrance Type: Eau de Toilette: The French dunes provided *DUNE'S* inspiration. An oceanic floral scent—one of nature's most serene and pure landscapes—the coastal dunes. Top floral notes of lily, wallflower, and peony combine with oceanic notes of broom, lichen, and amber.

Bottle Design: Symbolizing the natural, flowing curves of a dune landscape, the perfume is presented in an undulating glass bottle. The flacon is tinted a luminous shade of apricot evoking the shimmering radiance of sand. The rounded curves lend a nuance of feminine sensuality and is crowned with a glass stopper resembling a dew drop.

Package Design: The warm Persian orange packaging, inspired by the glow of the setting sun, completes the *DUNE* visual, and is marked with Christian Dior's signature oval medallion—a symbol of prestige and refinement.

Pictured Size: .17oz.

Dimensions: 2" h x 1-3/8" w

CPG: $9.00

Eau Sauvage®
Launch Date: 1966

Fragrance Type: Eau de Toilette: A cultivated, virile scent for the refined man, *EAU SAUVAGE* has a brisk and fresh presence. Citrus, herbs, and woody accents combine in a fragrance of discreet vigor.

Bottle Design: Rectangular flask with chiseled lines.

Pictured Size: .34oz.

Dimensions: 2-1/4" h x 1-1/4" w

CPG: $4.00

Fahrenheit®
Launch Date: 1988
Fragrance Type: Eau de Toilette: A dynamic meeting of extremes, *FAHRENHEIT* affirms a return to nature's pure, primary state. This men's fragrance fuses energy, space, and sensuality with woody and amber accents enlivened by light florals and a contrast of balsamic notes.
Bottle Design: The *Fahrenheit* bottle expresses an encounter between Art and the Universe: a harnessing of life forces which imprint their inner rhythms on the objects created to impart a natural order and balance in perfect communion with the universe.
Package Design: The *Fahrenheit* box projects the same vibrations around fundamental colors—red, yellow and blue—which illustrate the themes of Space and Energy with a graphic intensity totally in tune with today's artistic trends.
Pictured Size: .34oz.
Dimensions: 2-1/2" h x 1" w
CPG: $7.00

Miss Dior®
Launch Date: 1947
Fragrance Type: Perfume: Elegant and refined, *MISS DIOR* is an aldehydic floral scent with woodsy under notes. The classic chypre fragrance is ladylike and tailored, with a quiet exuberance that blooms continuously with the warmth of the skin. The creation of *MISS DIOR* replaced the "boudoir perfumes" which had been popular until that time.
Bottle Design: Amphora style bottle.
Pictured Size: .03oz.
Dimensions: 1-1/2" h x1/2" w
CPG: $35.00

Fun Facts
Miss Dior ®
Named in honor of Christian Dior's sister—Catherine.

Miss Dior®

Launch Date: 1947
Bottle Design: From the 1950s issue of Christian Dior's "Pebble Series." Round flat.
Package Design: Presented on cardboard flats with a black and white houndstooth background.
Pictured Size: .06oz.
Dimensions: 1-1/2" h x 1" w
CPG: $50.00

Miss Dior®

Launch Date: 1947
(1992—Relaunch of MISS DIOR—France and again in the United States in 1993 in select accounts)
Bottle Design: *MISS DIOR* is reborn in the purity of the bottle—with its authentic emblems, sober, refined, and extraordinarily modern. It was designed in 1949 by Mr. Guerry-Colas. Frosted finish creating a subtle lighting effect of opacity and transparency with the fragrance's color. The frosted effect is also very soft to the touch—a satin feel. The cap is a very pure geometric form as transparent as crystal. Glistening, it shines in contrast with the frosted effect of the bottle.
Pictured Size: .17oz.
Dimensions: 1-1/2" h x 1-1/4" w
CPG: $12.00

Poison®

Launch Date: 1985
Fragrance Type: Espirit de Parfum: A strikingly bold scent, *POISON* captures woman as enchantress. With spicy notes of Russian coriander, Malaysian pepper and Ceylonese cinnamon, *POISON* exudes temptation and mystery. Fruity notes of orange blossom and wild berries convey a mood of capricious seduction.
Pictured Size: .17oz.
Dimensions: 1-1/2" h x 1-1/4" w
CPG: $7.00

Tendre Poison®
"Dressed in Light"
Launch Date: 1994
Fragrance Type: Eau de Toilette: A joyful and vivid melody...a subtle harmony of soft, fresh floral notes that find voice in broad daylight. The vivacious opening notes of galbanum and zesty mandarin blossom into an elegant floral bouquet, with the fruity aroma of freesia entwined in delicate accents of orange blossom. As a finale, sandalwood and vanilla bring a subtle softness to the bouquet. A fresh and feminine fragrance that blooms with the day and dazzles until nightfall—charmingly enticing.
Bottle Design: An elegant, utterly feminine flacon that opens itself up to daylight in the clearest, freshest of greens...topped with a shimmering glass stopper.
Package Design: The carton is a vivid green with the look of moire (a fabric—such as silk—having a watered appearance) as luminous as the *TENDRE POISON* fragrance itself.
Pictured Size: .17oz.
Dimensions: 1-1/2" h x 1-1/4" w
CPG: $9.00

Fun Facts
Tendre Poison®
"*Tendre Poison* exists in one, and only one concentration: Eau de Toilette. The character of the fragrance ideally lends itself to the single concentration of Eau de Toilette. Since *Tendre Poison* is fresh and soft by nature, it doesn't need to be "lightened" into a cologne. Since it is a an every day, all-the-time, anytime fragrance, it is not meant for the intensity of a perfume."
Christian Dior Perfumes, 1995

Other Christian Dior Fragrances

Diorama®
Launch Date: 1949
Christian Dior Boutique on Avenue Montaigne is the only place in the world that this fragrance is available.

Diorling®
Launch Date: 1963
Christian Dior Boutique on Avenue Montaigne is the only place in the world that this fragrance is available.

Dior-Dior®
Launch Date: 1976 (Discontinued)
Fragrance Type: Spicy, fruity top notes are blended with exotic floral middle notes. Base notes are light powdery notes.

Diorella®
Launch Date: 1972
Fragrance Type: With the refreshing sparkle of citrus, *DIORELLA* is a playful scent for uninhibited moments. Its crisp, clean fruity notes convey a sense of leisure and insouciance.

Dioressence®
Launch Date: 1979
Fragrance Type: Mysterious and provocative, *DIORESSENCE* is a multi-flowered, Oriental fragrance laced with jasmine, violet, rosebud, and patchouli. Exotic notes of vanilla, clove, and sandalwood lend an exuberant quality to the scent.

Eau de Cologne Poison®
Launch Date: 1989

Eau Fraîche®
Launch Date: 1953

Eau Sauvage Extreme®
Launch Date: 1984

"Esprit de Parfum" Miss Dior®
Launch Date: 1982

Jules®
Launch Date: 1980
Fragrance Type: Patchouli, sage, and sandalwood.

CHRISTIAN LA CROIX
Parfums Christian La Croix

C'est la vie!®
Launch Date: 1986
Fragrance Type: Parfum: Floral
Pictured Size: .13oz.
Dimensions: 2" h x 1" w
CPG: $12.00

CLARINS
Jacques Courtin-Clarins
Clarins, Paris

ELYSIUM®
"Heaven on Earth"
Launch Date: 1993
Fragrance Type: Eau de Toilette Concentré—A
fresh blend of delicate florals for a distinctly
feminine appeal. Succulent hydra-fruits give the
fragrance its instant sparkle then blended with
woody under notes that are velvety and warm for a
lasting impression—it's "Heaven on Earth."
Bottle Design: Packaged in frosted white and sea-
mist green glass with a naturals inspired leaf
design.
Package Design: Packaged in white with a
naturals inspired leaf design.
Pictured Size: .17oz.
Dimensions: 3-1/4" h x 1" w
CPG: $15.00 (Not for individual sale • Customer
Gift)

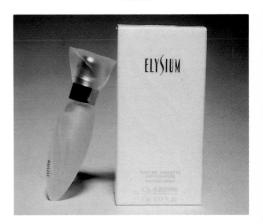

COTY

François Spoturno
Coty, Inc.

Emeraude®
Launch Date: 1923
Fragrance Type: Perfume: Distinctive and elegant oriental classic. Citrus and floral tops notes flow easily into soft floral middle notes. Base notes are warm and sweet with lasting power.
Pictured Size: .25oz.
Dimensions: 2-1/2" h x 1-1/4" w
CPG: $25.00

Emeraude®
Launch Date: 1923
Fragrance Type: Perfume
Pictured Size: .125oz.
Dimensions: 2" h x 1" w
CPG: $15.00 (Gift set)

L'Effleur®
"Somewhere inside romance blossoms."
Launch Date: 1990
Fragrance Type: Perfume: Fresh florals: The initial impression of this fragrance comes from unique top notes of green notes mixed with floral and fruity notes. The body is a rich floral bouquet and spices blended with base notes of woody, powdery notes that create a sensuous background.
Package Design: Designed exclusively for Coty by prominent graphic artist, Cynthia Hart.
Pictured Size: .125oz.
Dimensions: 2" h x 1-1/2" w
CPG: $15.00 (Gift set)

Fun Facts
L'Origan®
"Coty commissioned Bakst, the famous artist who earned his fame as the designer of stage settings and costumes for the first Ballet Russe to design the magnificent box covered with the "powder puff" paper which contains Coty's Airspun Face Powder. This design is currently being used today and the Airspun Face Powder is still scented with L'Origan fragrance."
Coty, Inc.

L'Origan®
Launch Date: 1907
Fragrance Type: Cologne: Means "The Golden One". This warm sensual fragrance is classified as a spicy-floral blend. The floral top note is enlivened by spices and a citrus bouquet. More flower oils make up the middle notes. Base notes emerge with warm, spicy, woody notes.
Pictured Size: .17oz.
Dimensions: 1-3/4" h x 1" w
CPG: $15.00-$20.00

La Rose Jacqueminot®
Launch Date: 1905
Fragrance Type: Cologne
Pictured Size: .27oz.
Dimensions: 2-1/4" h x 3/4" w
CPG: $65.00-$85.00

Lady Stetson®
"It's how the west was won."
Launch Date: 1986
Fragrance Type: Perfume: Aldehydic floral. A romantic floral bouquet that softens to deeper woodsy notes. Amber and mossy notes can also be found.
Pictured Size: .125oz.
Dimensions: 2" h x 1" w
CPG: $5.00

74

Longing®
"Make a Man Remember."
Launch Date: 1994
Fragrance Type: Perfume: Sheer Floriental. A new and innovative fragrance of extraordinary beauty that is dramatic, romantic, and emotionally compelling. This distinctive scent opens with a big bright sparkling top note designed to capture a breezy freshness through a "breezy fresh accord": coupled with hyacinth, muguet, violet, tagette, and osmanthus wrapped with the clear floralcy of freesia and mimosa head spaces (Givaudan-Roure captives) that lends a new signature to the composition, giving it a sophisticated and utterly feminine ciage. The enveloping top note weaves itself into a rich floral heart where a full bodied bouquet of jasmine, ylang-ylang, rose, orange flower, tuberose, and clove marries with sultry warmth of methyl ionones for a creamy, cozy and comfortable feeling. This exquisite profusion of floralcy is supported by an opulent floriental dry down composed of sandalwood reinforced with contemporary wood notes, amber, vanilla, and musk laced with exotic nuances of incense and oakmoss hereby completing the scent with warmth, mystery, and a romantic intensity that will leave a long lasting wake that becomes the memory of the wearer.
Bottle Design: The bottle and cap were designed by Jack Kingsbury.
Pictured Size: .125oz.
Dimensions: 1-1/2" h x 1-3/4" w
CPG: $15.00 (Gift set)

Masumi®
Launch Date: October, 1976
Fragrance Type: Parfum: Oriental-Floral bouquet. Florals and fruity notes create the top notes. Classic, elegant floral middle notes are blended with feminine mossy, powdery base notes.
Pictured Size: .25oz.
Dimensions: 2" h x 1-3/8" w
CPG: $5.00

75

Muguet des Bois®
Launch Date: 1936
Fragrance Type: Parfum de Toilette: Single-note floral. This extremely balanced composition reflects the delicate femininity of the Muguet flower. *It is one of the few fragrances whose top note is the same as its middle and final note.*
Package Design: Cynthia Hart redesigned *Muguet Des Bois* fragrance packaging. (Coty, 1994)
Pictured Size: .25oz.
Dimensions: 2-1/4" h x 1-1/4" w
CPG: $5.00

Nuance®
Launch Date: Late, 1975
Fragrance Type: Perfume: Contemporary floral bouquet. Top notes are citrusy and fruity. Middle notes are sweet and floral and blended to base notes that are warm, woody, and powdery.
Pictured Size: .12oz.
Dimensions: 2" h x 1" w
CPG: $4.00

Paris®
Launch Date: 1922
Fragrance Type: Parfum: Floral
Pictured Size: .16oz.
Dimensions: 2-1/2" h x 3/4" w
CPG: $15.00-$20.00

Sand & Sable®
Launch Date: 1981
Fragrance Type: Cologne: Modern floral blend. The body is a primarily floral. An intense diffusion from green top notes and citrusy notes blend smoothly into the floralcy. Sweet amber, woodsy, and musky base notes provides support and richness to the overall character.
Pictured Size: .25oz.
Dimensions: 2-1/8" h x 2-1/8" w
CPG: $6.00

Truly Lace®
Launch Date: 1992
Fragrance Type: Perfume: Floral Oriental. This distinctively feminine fragrance begins with a unique floralcy creating a deep sensuality. Top notes are a brilliant blend of living florals. The body is rich with a luxurious white floral bouquet. The romantic base notes are amber, woody, and powdery.
Package Design: Designed exclusively for Coty by prominent graphic artist, Cynthia Hart.
Pictured Size: .125oz.
Dimensions: 2-1/4" h x 1-1/2" w
CPG: $15.00 (Gift set)

Other Coty Fragrances

Chypre®
Launch Date: 1917
Fragrance Type: Floral-Spicy. Fresh fruit notes create the top notes. Middle notes are classic florals blended with warm, mossy base notes.

Complice®
Launch Date: 1978
Fragrance Type: Spicy and fruity notes create the top notes. Middle notes are sweet florals blended with warm, woody base notes.

Coty Musk® for Men
"what attracts?...this is what attracts."
Launch Date: 1974
Fragrance Type: A virile, exciting Oriental Musk blend. The oriental musk top note is accompanied by fresh citrus notes, and as it warms, the musk, amber, woody, and animalistic characteristics emerge and predominate through the middle and final notes.

!ex'cla.ma'tion®
"Make A Statement Without Saying A Word."
Launch Date: 1988
Fragrance Type: Cologne: This feminine floral-oriental consists of top notes that are herbaceous combined with luscious fruity, florals. The floral middle notes blend into a background of base notes that are amber, woody, and powdery.

Ghost Myst®
Launch Date: 1995
Fragrance Type: Transparent fresh floral. Sheer and fresh, the distinctive top note opens with the gently sparkling transparency of bergamot, mandarin, and cyclamen woven with refreshing watery notes of osmanthus headspace, a fresh berry accord and peach lending a lusciousness to the fragrance. This luscious signature extends into the heart note with sheer wet floralcy of freesia, muguet, jasmine, and magnolia headspace skillfully intertwined with elegant green floral notes of tagette and violet to add a simple sophistication that speaks to a woman's inner beauty. A soft modern backdrop composed of clear cedarwood and amber wrapped in a comfortable veil of sandalwood and musks rounds out this timely feminine fragrance.

Gravity®
"YOU COULDN'T RESIST IT, EVEN IF YOU TRIED"
Launch Date: 1992
Fragrance Type: Fresh, citrus, woody, oriental, and a marine tone give this fragrances its unique top note. Slight floral notes combined with woody notes create a very rich middle note. Base notes are warm and sweet.
Bottle Design: Patented bottle design by Raymond Bareiss.

ici®
Launch Date: 1995
Fragrance Type: Floral-Oriental: This mysterious fragrance experience begins with a unique top note of Living Magnolia and Rain Forest Orchid. The body combines beautiful floral notes of muguet, mimosa, and peony with a touch of spring hyacinth and orris; but the heart and soul of this scent comes from the deeply sensual and seductive, edible background. It has a blend of a creamy accord consisting of caramel, creme brulee, and cocoa. Amber, musk, and exotic woods create the dramatic and memorable theme of this new floral oriental scent.

Imprévu®
Launch Date: 1965
Fragrance Type: Modern floral blend, mossy, and flowery.

Iron®
Launch Date: 1987
Fragrance Type: Herbaceous, woody, fougère: Fresh green herbal top notes coupled with rich, woody middle notes. At the base is warm, woody notes that blend together to create a memorable impression.

L'Aimant®
(Means both "magnet" and "lover")
Launch Date: 1927
Fragrance Type: Eau de Toilette: Classic floral bouquet. Floral top notes are supported by aldehydic aromatics woody middle notes. Warm, woody classical base notes finalize one of Francois Coty's best-loved fragrances.

Preferred Stock®
"what preferred men prefer"
Launch Date: 1990
Fragrance Type: This herbaceous, woody, and green citrus masculine scent is a sophisticated blend that create the top notes. The body is warm and spicy with a herbaceous spice complex. Base notes are woody, deepened with moss and balsam and finished with musk and animal notes.

Sophia®
Launch Date: 1980
Fragrance Type: Perfume: Floral bouquet with oriental under notes.

Stetson®
Launch Date: 1981
Fragrance Type: Modern woody-citrusy bouquet. Provocative top notes of fresh citrus and florals blend into a spicy complex middle note enhanced by woody oils. The strength and lasting power of this masculine blend emerges in base notes that are animalic and woody.

Stetson Sierra®
Launch Date: 1993
Fragrance Type: Fresh, coniferous, woody, and fougère. The signature top notes reflect images of a mountain stream surrounded by deep, rich forests. This masculine feeling moves into the heart where it blends with a warm accord of tantalizing spices and clean woody under notes.

Final notes are balanced with precious, as well as modern, woods and warm, comfortable long-lasting notes creating an image of a forest hideaway.

Tribe®
Launch Date: 1991
Fragrance Type: This fruity, floral fragrance begins with fruity apricot blended into heart notes of rose and Amazon lily. Bottom notes are musky, mossy notes with the addition of florals and woody notes.

Vanilla Fields®
Launch Date: 1993
Fragrance Type: Floral-Oriental. The tops notes are rich vanilla, the heart of this creation, alivened with a spring floral bouquet and complemented with hints of sparkling citrus notes and light green qualities. Gently woven together the heart is a floral garland which surrounds the vanilla theme. Base notes are woody and blended with accents of amber, moss, and musk.

Vanilla Musk by Coty®
Launch Date: 1994
Fragrance Type: Perfume: Soft Oriental. This creation is a sensual fragrance based on a warm creamy combination of natural vanilla, musk and natural sandalwood. The initial burst and sparkle of this composition is achieved by a distinctive accord of bergamot, peach and mulberry. Added interest is given by the feminine floral notes of jasmine, rose, freesia, and muguet. Reinforced by a subtle cedarwood accord which provides transparency and modernity.

Wild Musk®
"Wild about You"
Launch Date: 1972
Fragrance Type: This oriental musk includes pleasurable hints of fresh citrus and vanilla with a floral musk. At the heart warmth emerges with floral and amber notes and blends into a final note of musk. The result is rich, warm and provocative.

**Special Note: Many of the earlier Coty fragrances were produced in glass bottles which were designed by the renowned jeweler and glass designer, Rene Lalique. (Coty, 1994)

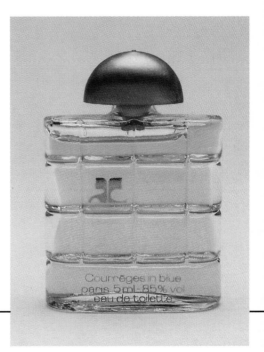

COURRÈGES
Andre Courrèges
Courrèges Parfums, Paris

Courrèges in Blue®
Launch Date: 1983
Fragrance Type: Parfum: Spicy top notes blended with floral middle notes and woody, powdery, and mossy base notes.
Bottle Design: Beveled, checkerboard squares set in a metal base with a gold dome stopper.
Package Design: Checkerboard squares in cool blue colors.
Pictured Size: .17oz.
Dimensions: 1-3/4" h x 1-1/4" w
CPG: $7.00

Other Courrèges Fragrances

Amérique®
Launch Date: 1974
Fragrance Type: Floral, fruity, and spicy.

Empreinte®
Launch Date: 1971
Fragrance Type: Chypre: Floral

Sweet Courrèges®
Launch Date: 1993
Fragrance Type: Floral

COVER GIRL

Incognito®
Launch Date: 1992
Fragrance Type: Cologne: Oriental: Ambered and spicy.
Bottle Design: Emerald green snap-on top accents the A-shaped frosted bottle with green lettering on front of bottle.
Pictured Size: .10oz.
Dimensions: 1-1/2" h x 1-1/8" w
CPG: $5.00

Navy®
Launch Date: 1990
Fragrance Type: Perfume: Oriental: Ambered and spicy.
Pictured Size: .10oz.
Dimensions: 1-1/2" h x 1-1/4" w
CPG: $5.00

Other Cover Girl Fragrances

Navy White®
Launch Date: 1994

DANA
Dana Perfumes Corp.

Herbissimo®
Launch Date: 1985
Fragrance Type: Cologne: Mountain juniper.
Pictured Size: .125oz.
Dimensions: 1-3/4" h x 1" w
CPG: $5.00

Tabu®
Launch Date: 1932 (1941 U.S.A.)
Fragrance Type: Perfume: Top notes of spicy oils
blend into a spicy, floral heart. Base notes are
warm, woody, and balsamic.
Pictured Size: .06oz.
Dimensions: 1-1/2" h x 3/4" w
CPG: $5.00

Fun Facts
Tabu®
First exhibited in 1901, Paris, Rene Prinet's painting *The Kreutzer Sonata* was
later acquired by the Spanish firm Dana and used to advertise *Tabu*.
"The Longest Kiss in History" is still used in Dana's ads (1995).

Ambush®
Launch Date: 1955
Fragrance Type: Eau de Perfume: Fresh, fruity top notes blended with floral middle notes. Base notes are sweet and powdery.

Ambush Tender Musk®
Launch Date: 1989

Canoe®
Launch Date: 1945
Fragrance Type: Citrusy top notes blend into middle notes of floral, woody notes. Base notes are sweet, powdery, and mossy.

Forbidden®
Launch Date: 1989

Musk Oil®
Launch Date: 1972

White Chantilly®
Launch Date: Fall, 1995
Fragrance Type: Chantilly's "little sister," this fragrance is a fruity, floral scent.

DANIEL DE FASSON
Parlux Fragrances, Inc.

Daniel de Fasson® Pour Femme
Launch Date: 1991
Fragrance Type: Parfum : Floral-Oriental.
Bottle Design: Bottle and cap have "pleating," giving effect of an open fan.
Package Design: Signature fan design in hot pink with red accents against a black background.
Pictured Size: .125oz.
Dimensions: 2- 1/2" h x 1-1/8" w
CPG: $12.00

Fun Facts
on Tenaz®

"Meaning 'tough and resourceful' reflects the spirit the fragrance and the man who wears it."
Parlux Fragrances

Tenaz®
Launch Date: 1994
Fragrance Type: Eau de Toilette: Woody-Fougère
Bottle Design: Strong, squared, masculine silhouette of frosted glass decorated with the Daniel de Fasson badge.
Package Design: Hand-painted picture frame of fiery red and explosive orange accents on a black background.
Pictured Size: .17oz.
Dimensions: 1-3/4" h x 1-3/8" w
CPG: $7.00

DECADENCE
Prince Matchabelli

***Decadence*®**
Launch Date: 1986 (Discontinued)
Fragrance Type: Eau de Toilette: Floral
Pictured Size: .125oz.
Dimensions: 2" h x 1-1/2" w
CPG: $10.00

DENEUVE
Catherine Deneuve

***Deneuve*®**
Launch Date: 1986
Fragrance Type: Parfum: Chypre
Pictured Size: .125oz.
Dimensions: 2" h x 1-1/8" w
CPG: $10.00

Deneuve®
Launch Date: 1986
Fragrance Type: Eau de Toilette
Pictured Size: .20oz.
Dimensions: 2" h x 1" w
CPG: $4.00

DIANA DE SILVA
Diana de Silva Cosmetiques Spa

Byblos®
Launch Date: 1992
Fragrance Type: Eau de Parfum: Floral-Fruity.
Bottle Design: Shape was inspired by the fluid curves of Phoenician amphora—round and short. The cap is a sculpted version of the Desert Rose.
Package Design: Sky blue, sea green, and desert sand colors design the outside packaging.
Pictured Size: .25oz.
Dimensions: 1-3/8" h x 1-3/8" w
CPG: $8.00

Genny Shine®
Launch Date: 1993
Fragrance Type: Eau de Toilette: Floral
Pictured Size: .17oz.
Dimensions: 1-1/2" h x 2" w
CPG: $7.00

Other Diana de Silva Fragrances

Byblos® for Men
Launch Date: 1995

Chiara Boni®
Launch Date: 1990
Fragrance Type: Floral

DIANE VON FÜRSTENBERG
Revlon, Inc.

Fun Facts
Doing it all and more:
A designer, an author, a mother, and a talk show hostess.

Tatiana®
Launch Date: 1975 (relaunched 1994)
Fragrance Type: Cologne: Named for her daughter. Flowery top notes with exotic floral heart notes blended with soft floral, powdery base notes.
Pictured Size: .07oz.
Dimensions: 1-1/4" h x 1-1/4" w
CPG: $5.00

Volcan d'Amour®
Launch Date: 1981
Fragrance Type: Top notes are fresh, floral and spicy. Middle notes are exotic floral blended with powdery, mossy, and ambered base notes.

DOLCE & GABBANA
Domenico Dolce and Stefano Gabbana

Dolce & Gabbana®
Launch Date: 1993
Fragrance Type: Eau de Toilette: Delicate notes of mandarin, freesia, and vanilla.
Pictured Size: .16oz.
Dimensions: 2" h x 1" w
CPG: $8.00

Other Dolce & Gabbana Fragrances

Fun Facts
Award Winner
1993 Italian Award winner for Best Woman's Fragrance.

Dolce & Gabbana® Pour Homme
Launch Date: March, 1995

DONNA KARAN
The Donna Karan Company

Donna Karan New York®
Launch Date: 1992
Fragrance Type: Perfume: Floral
Bottle Design: Designed by artist, sculptor, and husband of Donna Karan, Stephen Weis.
Pictured Size: .125oz.
Dimensions: 2-1/2" h x 1-1/8" w
CPG: $12.00

Other Donna Karan Fragrances

DK® for Men
Launch Date: 1994
Fragrance Type: Scents of suede and tobacco.

DOROTHY GRAY
Dorothy Gray Ltd.

Night Drums & Nose Gay®
Launch Date: 1930s
Pictured Size: .07oz. (each end)
Dimensions: 2-1/4" h x 3/4" w
CPG: $25.00

DRALLE
Georg Dralle

Illusion®
Launch Date: 1909
Pictured Size: .125oz.
Dimensions: 3-1/2" h x 1" w (Casing size)
CPG: $35.00-$50.00

Fun Facts
Tea Time!
In China, peony flowers are used to scent tea.

DUCHESS OF PARIS

Singapore Nights®
Launch Date: Undetermined
Pictured Size: .20oz.
Dimensions: 1-3/4" h x 1-1/2" w
CPG: $10.00 - $15.00

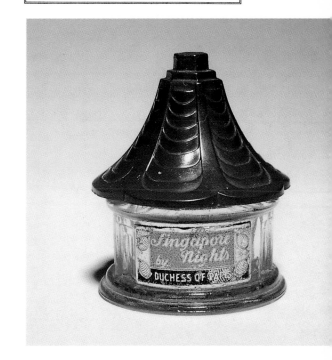

DUNHILL
Alfred Dunhill
Alfred Dunhill Limited

Blend 30®
Launch Date: 1979
Fragrance Type: Cologne: Was a rare and expensive blend of natural essences with a fresh patchouli and jasmine top note. As the fragrance developed on the wearer, a lush rosewood, balsam, nutty character evolves with hints of leather, cherry, and spicy herbs to give a long-lasting warm, floral fragrance.
Bottle Design: by Pierre Dinand.
Pictured Size: Photo courtesy of Alfred Dunhill Limited.

Fun Facts
Dunhill® for Men
"The design of its packaging was based on Alfred Dunhill's motoring accessory business—spiral shaped gear cog and wheel nuts."
Alfred Dunhill Limited

Dunhill® for Men
(formally known until 1979 as CLASSIC BLEND)
Launch Date: 1934
Fragrance Type: Cologne: Fougère: Woody-Ambered. Subtle yet crisp and clear in purpose has at first a fresh citrus note with lemon, lavender, and chamomile. It moves through a wood and musk phase with traces of spicy oils. Finally, it leaves an extremely long-lasting warm, amber scent.
Bottle Design: Designed by Mr. Donati with cap designed by Mr. George Sakier. Spiral shaped like a gear cog and the cap like wheel nuts.
Pictured Size: Photo courtesy of Alfred Dunhill Limited.

Dunhill Burgundy®
Launch Date: early 1980s
Fragrance Type: Eau de Toilette: Introduction canceled when a fragrance bearing a similar name appeared on the market. *No record of notes.*
Pictured Size: Photo courtesy of Alfred Dunhill Limited.

Dunhill Edition®
Launch Date: 1984
Fragrance Type: Eau de Toilette: Features a subtle yet distinctive fragrance. The top note evokes vital scents from Italy and Asia Minor: lemon, petit grain, bergamot, clary sage, and galbanum. The middle note is distinctive and masculine. Cloves from Madagascar, cardamom and cinnamon from Sri Lanka, and nutmeg contribute to its spicy, sensual character. The base note brings warmth and presence in a fusion of Indian sandalwood, labdanum, cedar wood, and hay oil.
Pictured Size: .17oz.
Dimensions: 2" h x 3/4" w
CPG: $5.00

Other Dunhill Fragrances

Dunhill London®
Launch Date: 1973
Fragrance Type: No record of notes.

ELIZABETH ARDEN
Florence Graham
Elizabeth Arden Co.

Blue Grass®
Launch Date: 1934
Fragrance Type: Perfume: Top notes are floral and citrus accords. Floral middle notes are blended with soft, powdery base notes.
Pictured Size: .25oz.
Dimensions: 1-3/4" h x 1-1/2" w
CPG: $6.00

Fun Facts
Blue Grass®
Florence Graham's most famous perfume was named for the sight of her Virginia retreat: Blue Grass.

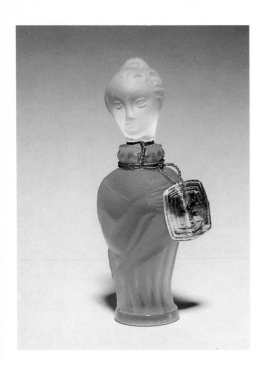

Mémoire Chérie®
Launch Date: 1949
Fragrance Type: Perfume: Herbaceous and floral notes.
Pictured Size: .25oz.
Dimensions: 3" h x 1" w
CPG: $325.00 (As Shown)

Red Door®
Launch Date: 1989
Fragrance Type: Perfume: Floral
Pictured Size: .17oz.
Dimensions: 2" h x 3/4" w
CPG: $7.00

Sunflowers®
Launch Date: 1993
Fragrance Type: Perfume
Pictured Size: .25oz.
Dimensions: 2- 1/8" h x 1-1/4" w
CPG: $7.00

True Love®
Launch Date: 1994
Fragrance Type: Perfume: Modern floral.
Pictured Size: .12oz.
Dimensions: 2-1/4" h x 1-3/8" w
CPG: $11.00

Other Elizabeth Arden Fragrances

Cabriole®
Launch Date: 1977
Fragrance Type: Citrusy

From Left to Right:
Diamonds & Emeralds®
1993: Floral bouquet.
Diamonds & Rubies®
1993: Floral-Oriental.
Diamonds & Sapphires®
1993: Green, fruity notes.
White Diamonds®
1991: Chypre
Pictured Size: .12oz.
Dimensions: 2" h x 1" w
CPG: $7.00 (each)

ELIZABETH TAYLOR

From Left to Right:
Diamonds & Emeralds®
1993: Floral bouquet.
Diamonds & Rubies®
1993: Floral-Oriental.
Diamonds & Sapphires®
1993: Green, fruity notes.
Passion®
1987: Chypre
White Diamonds®
1991: Chypre
Pictured Size: .17oz.
Dimensions: 1-1/2" h x 1-1/8" w
CPG: $5.00 (each)

Elizabeth Taylor's Passion®
Launch Date: 1987
Fragrance Type: Parfum: Chypre
Pictured Size: .12oz.
Dimensions: 2-1/4" h x 1-3/4" w
CPG: $7.00

Passion® For Men
Launch Date: 1989
Fragrance Type: Cologne: Oriental-Ambered.
Pictured Size: .20oz.
Dimensions: 1-3/4" h x 1-1/2" w
CPG: $7.00

Other Elizabeth Taylor Fragrances

Black Pearls®
Launch Date: 1995
Fragrance Type: Named after the black pearl.
Amber, sandalwood, and musk blended with
peach, gardenia, water lily, and white cloud rose.
Bottle Design: Frosted oyster shell-like bottle with
black pearl stopper.

ELVIS FRAGRANCES, INC.

Elvis®
Launch Date: 1992
Fragrance Type: Cologne
Pictured Size: .25oz.
Dimensions: 2-1/2" h x 1-1/4" w
CPG: $3.00

ENRICO COVERI

Paillettes®
Launch Date: 1984
Fragrance Type: Eau de Toilette
Pictured Size: .20oz.
Dimensions: 2" h x 1-3/4" w
CPG: $4.00

Fun Facts
A Soldier's Badge
Marigolds were worn as distinctive badges of honor by the Huguenot soldiers.

Erno Lazlo Inst. Ltd.

Evere®
Launch Date: August, 1989
Fragrance Type: Eau de Parfum
Pictured Size: .125oz.
Dimensions: 2-1/2" h x 1-3/4" w
CPG: $4.00

Escada Beaute Ltd.

Escada®
Margaretha Ley
Launch Date: 1990
Fragrance Type: Eau de Parfum: Floral-Oriental.
Bottle Design: Layered heart shaped clear glass
bottle. Cap is gold column-lined with red center on
top with plastic stopper.
Pictured Size: .14oz.
Dimensions: 2" h x 1-1/4" w
CPG: $10.00

Escada Acte 2®
Launch Date: 1995
Fragrance Type: Eau de Parfum: Elegant floral
bouquet of wild rose, peony, and freesia.
Bottle Design: Soft swirls that evoke images of
movement.
Pictured Size: .13oz.
Dimensions: 2-1/2" h x 3/4" w
CPG: $15.00 (Gift Set)

Other Escada Fragrances

Chiffon Sorbet®
Launch Date: 1993
Fragrance Type: This is a fruity, floral fragrance.
Bottle Design: Baby blue glass bottle with a silver ribbon top.

Escada® Pour Homme
Launch Date: 1993
Fragrance Type: Fresh-Oriental. Citrusy, spicy, and woody.

Ocean Blue®
Launch Date: 1995
Fragrance Type: Fruity-Floral. Designed and marketed as one of the "seasonal" fragrances.

Summer in Provence®
Launch Date: 1994

ESTEE LAUDER
Estee Lauder, Inc.

Aliage®
Launch Date: 1972
Fragrance Type: Eau de Parfum: Green notes with citrus oils are the top notes. Middle notes are spicy while base notes are mossy with hints of musk.
Pictured Size: .12oz.
Dimensions: 2-1/4" h x 3/4" w
CPG: $7.00

Azurèe®
Launch Date: 1969
Fragrance Type: Perfume: Herbaceous and floral notes create the top notes. The heart of this fragrance is floral. Base notes are woody, leathery, and warm.
Pictured Size: .12oz.
Dimensions: 2-1/4" h x 3/4" w
CPG: $7.00

Fun Facts
on Estee Lauder
She collects fine jeweled boxes and has used them as an inspiration for her glacés.

Beautiful®
Launch Date: 1985
Fragrance Type: Perfume: Floral
Pictured Size: .12oz.
Dimensions: 1-3/4" h x 1-1/2" w
CPG: $12.00

Cinnabar®
Launch Date: 1978
Fragrance Type: Eau de Parfum: Spicy oils and
fruity notes create the top notes. Middle notes are
spicy, exotic florals mingled with sensual, balsamic
base notes.
Pictured Size: .12oz.
Dimensions: 1-3/4" h x 1" w
CPG: $9.00

Estee®
Launch Date: 1968
Fragrance Type: Perfume: Fruity notes blended
with citrus oils create the top notes. Sweet floral
middle notes are combined with woody and
powdery base notes.
Pictured Size: .12oz.
Dimensions: 2-3/8" h x 1" w
CPG: $8.00

Knowing®
Launch Date: 1988
Fragrance Type: Parfum: Chypre-Floral.
Pictured Size: .12oz.
Dimensions: 1-3/8" h x 1-3/4" w
CPG: $12.00

Pleasures®
Launch Date: 1995
Fragrance Type: Perfume:
Delicate florals of white
lilies and peonies.
Pictured Size: .12oz.
Dimensions: 2-1/2" h x 3/4" w
CPG: $12.50

Private Collection®
Launch Date: 1973
Fragrance Type: Perfume: Fresh green notes and
citrus oils create the top notes. Floral middle notes
are blended with mossy, woody, and ambered base
notes.
Pictured Size: .07oz.
Dimensions: 1-3/4" h x 3/4" w
CPG: $10.00

Spellbound®
Launch: Date: 1991
Fragrance Type: Perfume: Floral
Pictured Size: .125oz.
Dimensions: 1-1/8" h x 1-1/8" w
CPG: $12.00

Tuscany Per Donna®

"Tuscany. Where a woman's presence is an inspiration. And the great art of life is love."
Launch Date: January, 1993
Fragrance Type: Parfum: Soft, romantic fragrance lush-blooming jasmine, fresh with Mediterranean herbs, softly sensual with amber and vanilla—the glowing warmth of a sunset over the Tuscan Hills of Italy.
Bottle Design: The bottle, with its soft, sensual curves in clear and frosted glass, is accented with the Tuscany Per Donna signature in script. Each bottle is molded with the Tuscany star, the renaissance symbol of Florentine glass makers, and is topped with the beautiful matte copper metallic cap with glossy collar.
Package Design: The carton is inspired by the sumptuous floral tapestries which have graced Tuscan villas. From inside the carton comes a soft glow of honey and cream tapestry.
Pictured Size: .12oz.
Dimensions: 1-1/4" h x 1-1/4" w
CPG: $18.00

Tuscany® Per Uomo

"IT MOVES THE SUN AND THE OTHER STARS. - DANTE"
Launch Date: 1994
Fragrance Type: Eau de Toilette: Fougère: woody-ambery.
Pictured Size: .25oz.
Dimensions: 2-1/4" h x 1-1/4" w
CPG: $15.00 (Gift Set-The Collection Set)

White Linen®
Launch Date: 1978
Fragrance Type: Perfume: Citrus oil and flowery notes define the top notes while exotic florals are at the heart. Base notes are ambered, sweet, and powdery.
Pictured Size: .09oz.
Dimensions: 1-1/2" h x 1-1/8" w
CPG: $11.00

Youth Dew®
Launch Date: 1953
Fragrance Type: Perfume: Oriental notes with sweet, powdery notes.
Bottle Design: Lotus bud.
Pictured Size: .12oz.
Dimensions: 2" h x 1" w
CPG: $10.00

F. MILLOT
F. Millot - Paris

Crêpe de Chine®
Launch Date: 1928 (1929 USA)
Fragrance Type: Parfum: Chypre-Floral.
Pictured Size: .06oz.
Dimensions: 1-1/8" h x 1" w
CPG: $25.00

FABERGÉ
Cheseborough-Ponds, Inc.

Brut®
Launch Date: 1964
Brut was originally launched by Fabergé in 1964 but joined the Cheseborough-Ponds family in 1989.
Fragrance Type: Cologne: Fougère
Pictured Size: .375oz.
Dimensions: 3-1/2" h x 1 " w
CPG: $3.00

From Left to Right:
Aphrodisia®
1932: Chypre
Tigress®
1938: Fruity-Floral.
Woodhue®
c1940: Spicy
Pictured Size: .5oz.
CPG: $3.00 ea.

McGregor®
Launch Date: Undetermined
Fragrance Type: Cologne
Pictured Size: .25oz.
Dimensions: 2" h x 1" w
CPG: $4.00

Other Fabergé Fragrances

Babe®
Launch Date: 1977
Fragrance Type: Fresh, fruity top notes have just
a hint of floral added to floral middle notes and
soft ambered, mossy, and powdery base notes.

Cellini® for Men
Launch Date: 1980
Fragrance Type: Fougère

Flambeau®
c1950

Kiku®
c1940

Strawhat®
1938

FAÇONNABLE
Albert Goldberg, Founder
Façonnable Parfums Paris

Façonnable®
Launch Date: 1995 U.S.A.
Fragrance Type: Eau de Toilette: The top notes are gloriously fresh, both spontaneous with gentian, wild mint, mandarin orange, and orange-flower, and energetic with new hedione (fresh jasmine petal) and ozone-fresh spearmint, marine notes, and watermelon. The middle notes develop this crystalline freshness with damascene rose, whose legendary elegance fuses with geranium and absolute of orange-flower to express the peerless refinement and authenticity of the *Façonnable* universe. The base is an invitation to a most masculine sensuousness with its woody fullness: sandalwood and cedar, underscored by musk and Moroccan amber, sublimely revealing the structural richness of the scent.
Bottle Design: Solid, structured, finely crafted, it evokes tradition and balance. Yet small details reveal that this harmony is a means of underscoring the originality of the concept: the metal cap is held in place by a leather thong encircling a bubble of glass. A new rendition of the tailor's thimble and the saddler's thong, a technical prowess that expresses the spirit of *Façonnable* with inimitable style.
Package Design: The box itself is an event in the world of fragrances; a metal case evocative of luxury cigar boxes or precious spice boxes that are treasured for years.
Pictured Size: Photo courtesy of Fragrance Marketing Group

DRESSING COMPLET POUR HOMME

FASHION TWO TWENTY

Perfume Number XI®
Launch Date: Undetermined
Fragrance Type: Perfume
Pictured Size: .07oz.
Dimensions: 1-3/8" h x 1" w
CPG: $2.00

FENDI

Asja®
Launch Date: 1991
Fragrance Type: Eau de Parfum: Oriental-Spicy.
Pictured Size: .17oz.
Dimensions: 1-1/2" h x 2-1/4" w
CPG: $8.00

Fendi®
Launch Date: 1985
Fragrance Type: Eau de Parfum: Chypre-Floral.
Pictured Size: .17oz.
Dimensions: 1-3/4" h x 1-1/2" w
CPG: $7.00

Fendi Uomo®
Launch Date: 1989
Fragrance Type: Eau de Toilette: Oriental-Woody.
Pictured Size: .17oz.
Dimensions: 1-1/2" h x 1-3/8" w
CPG: $7.00

Frances Denney

Hope®
Launch Date: c1950
Fragrance Type: Perfume: Aldehyde-Floral.
Pictured Size: .25oz.
Dimensions: 2-3/4" h x 3/4" w
CPG: $4.00

Interlude®
Launch Date: 1962
Fragrance Type: Perfume: Floral: Rose, jasmine, and orange flowers with patchouli, musk, and myrrh.
Pictured Size: .125oz.
Dimensions: 1-3/4" h x 3/4" w
CPG: $5.00

Fred Hayman
Parlux Fragrances, Inc.

> **Fun Facts**
> on Fred Hayman
> "Appointed as 'Fashion Consultant' for the Academy Awards."
> Parlux Fragrances, 1994

...with Love®
Launch Date: 1991
Fragrance Type: Perfume: Fruity-floral, oriental.
Bottle Design: A faceted crystal parallelogram shaped bottle.
Package Design: Mirrored gold parallelogram shaped box highlighted with red graphics.
Pictured Size: .125oz.
Dimensions: 1-3/8" h x 1-3/4" w
CPG: $15.00

273® for Women

"The sexiest women in Beverly Hills have Fred Hayman's number. 273."

Launch Date: 1989

Fragrance Type: Perfume: Floral oriental.

Bottle Design: Unique pyramid-shaped sculpted flacon with a red 273 logo.

Package Design: A vibrant yellow gift-wrapping presentation capturing the spirit and fun of Beverly Hills.

Pictured Size: .125oz.

Dimensions: 2-3/8" h x 1-1/2" w

CPG: $7.00

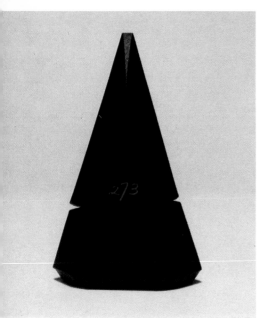

273® For Men

Launch Date: 1989

Fragrance Type: Exceptional Cologne: Woody-Chypre.

Bottle Design: Designed as a piece of art, it is a sculptured, pyramid of matte black glass accented with a red 273 logo.

Package Design: Matte black with Fred Hayman red accents gift-wrapped presentation.

Pictured Size: .125oz.

Dimensions: 2-3/8" h x 1-1/2" w

CPG: $7.00

Fred Hayman's Touch®
"it all begins with touch"
Launch Date: 1993
Fragrance Type: Perfume: Floral-Oriental.
Bottle Design: Classic perfume design of cap and bottle, enhanced with Fred Hayman's gold initial seal.
Package Design: Irresistibly touchable, corduroy-like red box with a signature yellow border and gold trim.
Pictured Size: .125oz.
Dimensions: 2" h x 1" w
CPG: $15.00

GABRIELA SABATINI
Richard Barrie Fragrances, Inc.

Gabriela Sabatini®
Launch Date: 1991
Fragrance Type: Eau de Toilette: Created by 4711 Parfum Fabrik, Cologne, Germany. The top note, a burst of orange flower, jasmine, tuberose, and muguet, gives way to a fruity blend of carnation and cedarwood. Anchoring the scent is a powdery base of vanilla and heliotrope.
Bottle Design: A slim and graceful clear glass bottle displays a gentle swirl which takes its cue from Sabatini's name. The sculpted lines continue to the bottle's frosted top which bears the initials "GS" printed in gold and fashioned to resemble a tennis ball.
Package Design: A deep purple box accented with light purple lines and touches of gold conveys the scent's dynamic and youthful energy.
Pictured Size: .10oz.
Dimensions: 1-3/8" h x 1-1/4" w
CPG: $12.00

Magnetic®

Launch Date: 1993

Fragrance Type: Eau de Toilette The fruity elements heighten the lively and fresh top note which unfolds to a lively floral bouquet. The addition of precious woods and subtle balsamic elements intensify to create a sensuous and intriguing fragrance —a fragrance that captures the fire of emotion.

Bottle Design: Designed with romance in mind, it entices the emotions of all who touch it.

Package Design: Packaged in a fiery, exotic red design to encourage excitement.

Pictured Size: .10oz.

Dimensions: 1-1/2" h x 1-1/2" w

CPG: $5.00

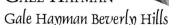

Gale Hayman

GALE HAYMAN
Gale Hayman Beverly Hills

Gale Hayman Beverly Hills®

Launch Date: Spring, 1990

Fragrance Type: Perfume: Oriental

Bottle Design: Rock shaped bottle with plastic snow leopard snap-on stopper. The majestic snow leopard symbolizes today's woman—powerful grace. Name on front in gold tone lettering.

Pictured Size: .10oz.

Dimensions: 1-1/8" h x 1-1/2" w

CPG: $10.00

Delicious® by Gale Hayman

Launch Date: Summer, 1993

Fragrance Type: Perfume: Sensual florals blended with alluring and exotic powdery, woody notes.

Bottle Design: Rock shaped bottle with plastic snow leopard stopper. The leopard symbolizes today's woman—powerful grace.

Pictured Size: .10oz.

Dimensions: 1-1/8" h x 1-1/2" w (side view)

CPG: $10.00

Fun Facts
on Gale Hayman
"Gale Hayman is the co-creator of the Giorgio Beverly H▮
boutique and Giorgio perfume."
Gale Hayman Beverly Hills

Geoffrey Beene

Grey Flannel®
Launch Date: 1976
Fragrance Type: Eau de Toilette: Chypre
Pictured Size: .5oz.
Dimensions: 2-3/4" h x 1" w
CPG: $5.00

Other Geoffrey Been Fragrances

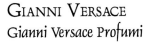

Bowling Green®
Launch Date: 1986
Fragrance Type: Fougère

Chance®
Launch Date: 1994
Fragrance Type: Parfum: A fruity, floral fragrance.
Bottle Design: Lunar elliptical rounded black, white, and gold bottle.

Red®
Launch Date: 1976
Fragrance Type: Perfume: Top notes are citrusy and spicy with elegant floral middle notes. Base notes are mossy and woody.

Gianni Versace
Gianni Versace Profumi

Versace® L'Homme
Launch Date: October, 1984
Fragrance Type: Eau de Toilette: Chypre-Leathery.
Pictured Size: .17oz.
Dimensions: 2" h x 1" w
CPG: $8.00

Versus® Uomo
Launch Date: March, 1991
Fragrance Type: Eau de Toilette: Chypre-Leathery
Pictured Size: .125oz.
Dimensions: 1-3/4" h x 1-1/8" w
CPG: $6.00

V'E Versace®
Launch Date: 1989
Fragrance Type: Eau de Parfum: V'E Versace is an exciting blend of elegance and a new sensuality. The top note is an evocative harmony of precious white florals—lily of the valley, ylang-ylang, jasmine, lily, and Bulgarian rose blended with the essence of bergamot. The heart of the fragrance moves to a harmony of orange blossoms and iris to reveal the final, sensual notes of balsamic wood, incense, amber, and sandalwood.
Bottle Design: A cube which is not a cube...an object of surprising, unsettling beauty. Totally modern. A future classic. Its form is an expression of graceful symmetry with a series of deliberately asymmetrical elements. Versace wanted something that would become a symbol.
Pictured Size: .125oz.
Dimensions: 1-3/8" h x 3/4" w
CPG: $9.00

Versus Donna®
Launch Date: February, 1992
Fragrance Type: Eau de Toilette: Proud, unique, sensual, and inebriating, the fragrance combines the fascination richness of the flower notes with the fragrances of musk and wood, honeysuckle, jonquil, lavender and ylang-ylang making for an extraordinary dominant floral notes. The VERSUS women's fragrance is pure liquid style and flawlessly captures the VERSUS woman: electrifying, sensual, and habitually unattainable.
Bottle Design: This sleek and striking, triangular bottle consists of both angular and bowed contours which form a "V" on the face. V for VERSUS. V for VERSACE. Composed of ruby red glass with a gold collar and a lipstick red cap, the design is dramatic and powerful. The base of the bottle becomes a massive crystal prism to counterbalance with its transparency, the amber color of the liquid fragrance.
Package Design: The carton is composed on all four sides by a single photograph, tinted ruby red. When the cartons are displayed collectively at varying angles, a complete photographic image unfolds to reveal an oblong masterpiece. The result is stunning...a dramatic look at a woman

who creates her own rules and forges her own path...a contrast between international super model, Carla Bruni, as the dynamic, daring *VERSUS* woman and six virile, aloof young men.
Pictured Size: .125oz.
Dimensions: 1-3/4" h x 1" w
CPG: $8.00

Other Versace Fragrances

Blonde®
Launch Date: 1995
Fragrance Type: Parfum: Floral
Bottle Design: Designed by Gianni Versace.

Blue Jeans & Red Jeans®
Launch Date: 1994

Gianni Versace®
Launch Date: 1982
Fragrance Type: Parfum: Chypre: Floral
Bottle Design: Bottle and stopper signify uncut diamonds and the metal collar is engraved with flower petals.

Fun Facts
on V'E VERSACE® Baccarat Crystal
"The cube is made of solid Baccarat Crystal and contains a smaller cube of perfume. Each Baccarat is hand crafted, signed and numbered. Only 250 bottles will be produced. The inspiration came from a solid crystal inkwellGianni Versace utilizes when working on his creations."
Fragrance Marketing Group

GILLES CANTUEL
Parfums Gilles Cantuel

Alamo®
Launch Date: Undetermined
Fragrance Type: Eau de Toilette
Pictured Size: .17oz.
Dimensions: 2-3/8 " h x 1" w
CPG: $6.00

Creature®
Launch Date: 1987
Fragrance Type: Eau de Toilette
Pictured Size: .15oz.
Dimensions: 2-3/4 " h x 1-1/8" w
CPG: $11.00

GIORGIO ARMANI

Armani® Eau Pour Homme
Launch Date: 1984
Fragrance Type: Chypre: Fresh: Bergamot and lavender, vetiver and sandalwood.
Pictured Size: .33oz.
Dimensions: 2-1/4" h x 1-1/2" w
CPG: $5.00

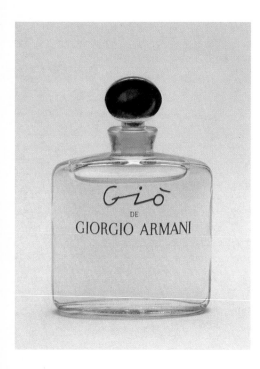

Giò®
Launch Date: 1992
Fragrance Type: Eau de Parfum: Florals and fruits with woody and spicy notes.
Pictured Size: .17oz.
Dimensions: 2" h x 1-1/4" w
CPG: $8.00

Other Giorgio Armani Fragrances

Armani®
Launch Date: 1982
Fragrance Type: Chypre: Fresh, fruity top notes are blended with florals and base notes that are woody and mossy.

Acqua di Giò®
Launch Date: 1995

GIORGIO BEVERLY HILLS

Giorgio Beverly Hills® For Women
Launch Date: 1981
Fragrance Type: Perfume: Sensuous, romantic florals blended with notes of sandalwood and patchouli.
Pictured Size: .12oz.
Dimensions: 2-1/4" h x 3/4" w
CPG: $9.00

V.I.P. Special Reserve®
Launch Date: 1982
Fragrance Type: Eau de Toilette: Oriental-Woody.
Pictured Size: .125oz.
Dimensions: 2-1/4" h x 1" w
CPG: $7.00

Red®
Launch Date: 1988
Fragrance Type: Perfume: A balanced formulation of floral, fruity, oriental, and chypre notes. Base notes are ambered, woody, spicy notes all blended for a memorable and distinctive creation. A totally new fragrance category called FLEURIFFE CHYPRE.
Pictured Size: .125oz.
Dimensions: 3 " h x 1" w
CPG: $11.00

Red® for Men
"PURE ATTRACTION"
Launch Date: 1989
Fragrance Type: Cologne: Wildflowers and citrus notes are added to the scent of spearmint oil. The heart emerges with "Living Nature" woody notes and florals. The base notes are a combination of ambered, woody, mossy notes. (Notes of "living nature include ebanol, orchids vanille, and warm vanilla.) Wonderfully masculine and earthy.
Bottle Design: Handsomely contained in a modern, masculine French-glass bottle and accented with a granite-gray cap, banded with a splash of red.
Pictured Size: .5oz.
Dimensions: 1-3/4 " h x 2-1/2" w
CPG: $7.00

Fun Facts
Red®
"RED is unlike any existing fragrance...its uniqueness stems from a scientifically advanced achievement called "Living Flower Technology." This breakthrough process captures the scent of living flowers at their fragrance peak..."
Giorgio Beverly Hills

Wings®
"SET YOUR SPIRIT FREE"

Launch Date: 1993

Fragrance Type: Perfume: Brilliant Floriental. Exotic living florals delicately blended with ambered, woody and powdery base notes.

Bottle Design: Smooth, round, and a perfectly symmetrical form. The stopper, a perfect sphere flushed in transparent blue, strikes a dramatic captivating balance with the free flowing, curvaceous bottle.

Package Design: Encased in a triangular box splashed with colorful sky blue, purple, green, celestial yellow, the overall effect is one of earth and sky.

Pictured Size: .125oz.

Dimensions: 1-3/4" h x 1-1/4" w

CPG: $15.00

Other Giorgio Beverly Hills Fragrances

Giorgio Beverly Hills® For Men
Launch Date: 1984

Fragrance Type: Blends of herbaceous, spicy notes with an accent of mandarin oil. The entire fragrance is accented with woody, spicy notes and is designed to "...distinctively smell like the well-dressed man."

Wings® for Men
Launch Date: 1994

GIVENCHY
Parfums Givenchy, Inc.
Hubert de Givenchy

Amarige®
Launch Date: 1991

Fragrance Type: Parfum: Head notes are fruity, floral, green notes blended with a bouquet of flowery, woody heart notes. Base notes are woody and ambered.

Bottle Design: Heart-like shaped bottle with a wide collar. The body of the bottle is clear glass with a plastic frosted flame stopper.

Package Design: The inspiration is red for romance and sensuality and yellow for exuberance, youth, and happiness. And an added touch of true green and dynamic blue create a joyful color combination in the spirit of a true master of style.

Pictured Size: .14oz.

Dimensions: 2-1/8" h x 1" w

CPG: $11.00

Eau De Givenchy®
Launch Date: 1980
Fragrance Type: Eau de Toilette: Floral-Fruity.
Pictured Size: .125oz.
Dimensions: 2" h x 3/4" w
CPG: $7.00

Insense®
Launch Date: 1993
Fragrance Type: Eau de Toilette: Woody, floral, and amber, this fragrance is full of fantasy and extravagance.
Bottle Design: The bottle is designed in the spirit of Amarige. The curves are simple, without angles or rigidity. A matte silver snap-on cap highlights the asymmetric shape.
Package Design: Vibrant yellow rarely used in most men's fragrances. Vivid yellow bordered in dynamic blue, a symbol of enthusiasm, energy, and optimism. An important accent of green adds vivacity, a sense of nature and freshness. The silver lines bring an added touch of elegance and refinement.
Pictured Size: .25oz.
Dimensions: 2-1/8" h x 1-1/4" w
CPG: $8.00

Le De Givenchy®
Launch Date: c1965
Fragrance Type: Parfum: Fresh florals and spicy accents define the top notes. At the heart delicate florals blend with soft powdery base notes.
Pictured Size: .06oz.
Dimensions: 1-3/4" h x1" w
CPG: $6.00

YSATIS®
Launch Date: 1984
Fragrance Type: Parfum: Floral, cypress and oriental all at once.
Bottle Design: Created by Pierre Dinand. Clear, glass bottle that is vertical and slender—it conjures up the wild allure of a silhouette. The deep-set facets mirror the complexity of the fragrance. The plastic stopper, pyramid shaped, is dramatically cut like a crystal sculpture. The lines of the bottle capture a certain rhythm—a form of beauty.
Pictured Size: .125oz.
Dimensions: 2-1/8" h x 3/4" w
CPG: $7.00

Xeryus®

Launch Date: 1986
Fragrance Type: Eau de Toilette: A bouquet of flowers opening out on a woody-spiced background.
Bottle Design: Created by Pierre Dinand. Rectangular architectural shape. The glass is rich steel gray and iridescent. Gold lettering compliments Dinand's art.
Package Design: The packaging of *XERYUS* is designed as a sculpture. Created by Pierre Dinand.
Pictured Size: .14oz.
Dimensions: 1-3/4" h x 1" w
CPG: $7.00

Other Givenchy Fragrances

Givenchy 111®
Launch Date: 1970
Fragrance Type: Precious florals blended with woody, mossy notes.
Fragrance Philosophy: The Givenchy III woman dreams of embodying refinement, balance, good taste, absolute elegance. She emphasizes the essential things in life.

L'Interdit®
Launch Date: 1957
Fragrance Type: Parfum: Fruity defines the top notes with elegant classic florals at the heart. Base notes are sensual, powdery, and balsamic notes.
Fragrance Philosophy: The L'Interdit woman dreams of being attractive, romantic, tender, passionate. She is feminine, graceful, light hearted. She is eternally feminine, likes to wear organza, lace, velvet.

Monsieur de Givenchy
Launch Date: 1959
Fragrance Type: Citrusy tops notes blended with elegant classic florals at the heart. Base notes are sensual musk and mossy notes.
Fragrance Philosophy: The Monsieur de Givenchy man is a traditionalist, seeking harmony and authenticity. He prefers originals to imitations. His motto: Elegance. Quite simply, he loves quality.

Givenchy Gentleman
Launch Date: 1975
Fragrance Philosophy: The Givenchy gentleman man is decisive and sure of himself. A contemporary man who likes modern accessories and objects. He wears unexpected combinations of fabrics and colors.

Ptisenbon de Tartine and Chocolat
Launch Date: 1987
Fragrance Philosophy: The name became an undisputed favorite with children. The personality is light, mischievous, gentle, tender. Pure freshness.

GLORIA VANDERBILT

Glorious®
Launch Date: 1987
Fragrance Type: Perfume: Floral
Pictured Size: .125oz.
Dimensions: 2-3/8" h x 1-1/4" w
CPG: $5.00

V®
Launch Date: 1994
Fragrance Type: Eau de Toilette: Modern floral. *V* uses living flower technology with hyacinth and freesia. Sandalwood warms this scent.
Pictured Size: .25oz.
Dimensions: 2-3/4" h x 1" w
CPG: $5.00

Other Gloria Vanderbilt Fragrances

Vanderbilt®
Launch Date: 1981
Fragrance Type: Eau de Parfum: Classic and elegant this light, flowery scent begins to mingle with middle notes of exotic florals and sweet, powdery, oriental base notes.

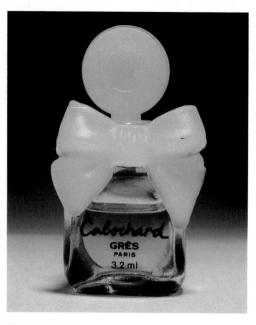

GRÈS
Alix Barton Parfums Grès
Lippens Inc. International

Cabochard®
(Obstinate)
Launch Date: 1959
Fragrance Type: Parfum: Innovative right from its very creation, *Cabochard* was daring enough to carry a masculine name and resolutely new "floral chypre" avant-grade olfactory note. A sensual and heady perfume with a unique subtle mix of floral, woody, and lichens notes. *Just one ounce of Cabochard takes 6,400 jasmine flowers, 240 Bulgarian roses and more than 10 ingredients.*
Bottle Design: For Cabochard's 25th anniversary (1984/85), the famous gray velvet bow is immortalized in molded glass.
Pictured Size: .12oz.
Dimensions: 2" h x 1" w
CPG: $9.00

Fun Facts
on Cabochard®
"In 1956, Madame Grès was chosen by the FORD foundation to travel to India to study the best way to adapt India weaving techniques to the western market. Fascinated by all the new, rare and exotic fragrances she discovered, she decided to create a perfume to be offered to women as a new accessory. In 1959, she launched her first perfume, Cabochard® ."
Lippens Inc. International

Cabotine® de Grès
Launch Date: 1990
Fragrance Type: Eau de Parfum: A floral fragrance synchronized around a rare flower, the Ginger Lily.
Bottle Design: By Thierry Lecoule.
Package Design: By Thierry Lecoule.
Pictured Size: .12oz.
Dimensions: 2 " h x 1" w
CPG: $10.00

Other Grès Fragrances

Alix®
Launch Date: 1982
Fragrance Type: Cultured, floral, and green notes are blended to create this ageless fragrance.

Fun Facts
on Cabotine®
"International Award for the best female fragrance-1992; Academia del Profumo-Bologna (Italy) at Cosmoprof."
Lippens Inc. International

GUCCI
Gucci Parfums, Ltd.

Eau de Gucci®
Launch Date: 1982
Fragrance Type: Eau de Parfum: Floral bouquet with woody base notes.
Pictured Size: .25oz.
Dimensions: 2" h x 1-1/8" w
CPG: $5.00

Gucci No. 3®
Launch Date: 1985
Fragrance Type: Parfum: Florals
Pictured Size: .12oz.
Dimensions: 1-3/4" h x1" w
CPG: $6.00

Other Gucci Fragrances

Gucci Accenti®
Launch Date: 1995

Gucci Parfum 1®
Launch Date: 1972
Fragrance Type: Flowery top notes blended with spicy, floral middle notes and powdery, feminine base notes.

Gucci® Pour Homme
Launch Date: 1976
Fragrance Type: Chypre-Leathery.

Gucci Nobile®
Launch Date: 1988
Fragrance Type: Fougère

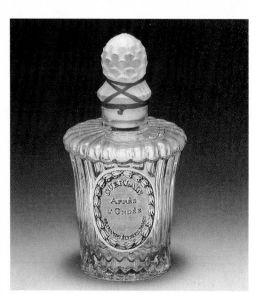

GUERLAIN
Founded by Pierre-François-Pascal Guerlain   Guerlain, Inc.

Après L'Ondée®
Launch Date: 1906
Fragrance Type: Perfume: Floral. (Jacques Guerlain). This delicate fragrance is a floral bouquet of violet, jasmine, carnation, and iris. "After the Rain," this fresh, delicate scent evokes the image of strolling in the wooded pathways in France on moist dewy mornings. *Après L'Ondée* was created for a woman with indefinable charm and tenderness.
Package Design: By Raymond Guerlain.
Pictured Size: Photo courtesy of Guerlain, Inc.

Fun Facts
on Guerlain Fragrances
"The oldest family-run fragrance and cosmetic company in the world, Guerlain has been creating quality products since its founding in 1828. During the last 165 years, more than 300 fragrances have been developed, every one a creation of a family member."
Guerlain, Inc.

Chamade®
Launch Date: 1969
Fragrance Type: Perfume: Semi-Oriental and floral fragrance of rose, jasmine, hyacinth, and vanilla. (Jean-Paul Guerlain). This ultra-feminine perfume was inspired by the liberated woman portrayed by Catherine Deneuve in the Film version of Francois Sagan's novel, *La Chamade*. A penetrating blend that exudes confidence and exoticism, Chamade emanates modern and vibrant charm. Chamade means "beating of the heart."
Bottle Design: The bottle design is an interpretation of the perfume's name *"Chamade,"* which means "The wild beating of the heart." The fluted glass body of the bottle is shaped into the form of an inverted heart, because according to theory, the woman who wears *Chamade*, turns men's hearts upside down! The stopper is said to derive from a teardrop shape; *Chamade* makes men weep with joy.
Package Design: By Raymond Guerlain.
Pictured Size: .07oz.
Dimensions: 2-1/4" h x 1-1/8" w
CPG: $15.00

Chant D'Arômes®

Launch Date: 1962

Fragrance Type: Perfume: Flowery and woody, the dominant notes are gardenia, rose, jasmine, honeysuckle, and ylang-ylang. (Jean-Paul Guerlain). Audrey Hepburn in *Roman Holiday*, Leslie Caron in *Gigi*—the youthful exuberance of these women inspired this fragrance of innocence and spring blossoms. Translated "A Song of Fragrance," *Chant D'Arômes*, which is composed of more than 55 ingredients, is for a woman with a discreet and charming personality.

Bottle Design: Now available in perfume . The *Chant d'Arômes* perfume bottle was designed to embody the woman who inspired the fragrance. The smooth delicacy of a debutante, the innocence of first love, this bottle evokes the simple white ball gowns worn during a young woman's entrance into society; the velvet ribbon around the collar serves as her only ornamentation.

Package Design: By Raymond Guerlain.

Pictured Size: Photo courtesy of Guerlain, Inc.

Eau de Cologne du Coq®

Launch Date: 1894

Fragrance Type: Eau de Cologne: Eau Fraîche. (Jacques Guerlain). Dry, fresh and invigorating, *Eau de Cologne du Coq* is sharp and delicate, composed of lemon and hesperides. *Eau de Cologne Coq* features the vitality of joyful awakenings—perfect for anyone at anytime.

Bottle Design: Created for the Imperiale Court, the distinctive glass bottle is covered in detailed relief with golden bees representative of the Napoleonic Crest that symbolize strength, resilience, and richness. The bottle is topped with a distinctive gold dome and a uniquely crafted transparent spherical stopper.

Pictured Size: .25oz.

Dimensions: 2-1/4 " h x 1" w

CPG: $7.00

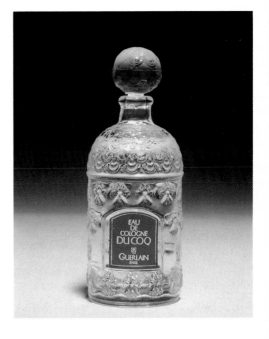

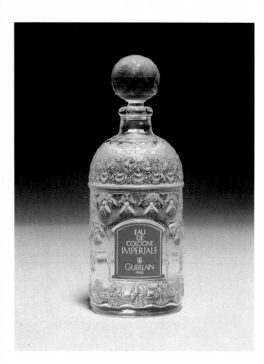

Eau de Cologne Impériale®
Launch Date: 1853
Fragrance Type: Eau de Cologne: Eau Fraîche.
(Pierre-Francois-Pascal Guerlain). *Eau de Cologne Impériale* is a royal bouquet of hesperides, orange blossom, rosemary, and neroli. *Eau de Cologne Impériale* was created for the Empress Eugenie, wife of Napoleon III. So impressed was the Empress by the refined fragrance, she bestowed Guerlain with the title "Her Majesty's Official Perfumer," the highest royal patent. *This is the oldest Guerlain fragrance still being sold today.*
Bottle Design: The glass flacon was a tribute to the royal court, etched in a "bee" motif reminiscent of the Napoleonic family crest that symbolizes strength, resilience, and richness. The bottle is topped with a distinctive gold dome and a uniquely crafted transparent spherical stopper. The label features the emblem of the Napoleonic crest; Guerlain alone is entitled to use this design.
Pictured Size: .25oz.
Dimensions: 2-1/4" h x 1" w
CPG: $7.00

Eau de Fleurs de Cédrat®
Launch Date: 1920
Fragrance Type: Eau de Toilette: Eau Fraîche: (Jacques Guerlain) *Eau de Fleurs de Cedrat* is sharp and fresh with bergamot and citrus top notes. This subtle, fruity fragrance captures the magic of the Mediterranean countries. Refreshing and invigorating at any time of the day, *Eau de Fleurs de Cedrat* is worn by both men and women.
Bottle Design: The distinctive glass bottle is covered in detailed relief with golden bees representative of the Napoleonic Crest that symbolize strength, resilience, and richness. The bottle is topped with a distinctive gold dome and a uniquely crafted transparent spherical stopper.
Pictured Size: Photo courtesy of Guerlain, Inc.

124

Eau de Guerlain®
Launch Date: 1974
Fragrance Type: Eau de Toilette: Eau Fraîche:
(Jean-Paul Guerlain) Dominant notes are citrus,
mint, tarragon, hesperides, neroli, thyme, and
lavender. In 1974 Guerlain created a fragrance of
such perfection and originality that it bears the
company name—*Eau de Guerlain*. Like the sea,
this fragrance is both refreshing and deep, ideal
for either men or women.
Bottle Design: The distinctive glass bottle is
covered in detailed relief with golden bees
representative of the Napoleonic Crest that
symbolize strength, resilience, and richness. The
bottle is topped with a distinctive gold dome and a
uniquely crafted transparent spherical stopper.
Pictured Size: .25oz.
Dimensions: 2-1/4 " h x 1" w
CPG: $7.00

Habit Rouge®
Launch Date: 1965
Fragrance Type: Eau de Toilette: Oriental, Woody.
Dominant notes are hesperides, woods, vanilla,
and patchouli. *Habit Rouge* meaning "riding coat,"
is based on an old French saying: "A woman is
chased and chased by a man until she catches
him." A fragrance that is as appealing and
rewarding to the men who wear it as it is to their
female companions, *Habit Rouge* is bold and
adventurous.
Package Design: By Raymond Guerlain.
Pictured Size: Photo courtesy of Guerlain, Inc.
CPG: $8.00

Héritage®
Launch Date: 1992

Fragrance Type: Eau de Toilette: Woody, spicy, and fresh. Since 1828, descendants of Pierre-Francois-Pascal Guerlain have perpetuated the traditions of the House, drawing on the past to ensure a successful future. Guerlain celebrates this rich history with *Héritage*, by Jean-Paul Guerlain. A fresh and exuberant fragrance of passion, authenticity, and quality, *Héritage* is for the man of tradition who looks to the future.

Bottle Design: The *Héritage* bottle was designed by sculptor and long-time Guerlain collaborator Robert Granai. The pendulum, designed by French physicist Foucault, served as the initial inspiration for the bottle. According to Granai, "The eternal quality of time represented by the pendulum metaphorically defines man's ancestral heritage and endurance." The spherical golden cap banded in black is an interpretation of Foucault's experimental pendulum that hung from the dome of the Pantheon. The transparent glass bottle has columnar, prismatic sides emerging from a keystone in the center.

Package Design: By Robert Granai. A matte and glossy rust-colored carton further reinforces the architectural package design.

Pictured Size: .13oz.

Dimensions: 1-3/4 " h x 1-3/4" w

CPG: $10.00

Jardins de Bagatelle®
Launch Date: 1983

Fragrance Type: Eau de Toilette: (Jean-Paul Guerlain). Floral. White floral bouquet: rose, jasmine, neroli, tuberose, and gardenia, balanced with an airy scent of orange blossom oil and a base of wood. *Jardins de Bagatelle*, a fragrance of purely white flowers, was inspired by the little white chateau in the Bois de Boulogne. The legend of the romantic Bagatelle retreat dates back to when the Count of Artois (brother of Louis XVI), and Queen Marie Antoinette made a wager in the Bois de Boulogne. While riding on horseback, he stopped at the site of a decrepit chalet and bet the queen that he would build a folly on the site in less than ten weeks. In 64 days, Bagatelle was built.

Bottle Design: Inspired by the Chateau Bagatelle, the columnar bottle reinforces the architecture of the building.

Package Design: By Robert Granai.

Pictured Size: Photo courtesy of Guerlain, Inc.

Jicky®
Launch Date: 1889

Fragrance Type: Perfume: Semi-Oriental. (Aimé Guerlain). Lavender, spices, hesperides, lemon, rosemary, vanilla, tonka bean, and a hint of musk interplay in this fragrance of contrasts. Considered the world's first modern perfume, Jicky was a labor of love for Aimé Guerlain. He created the fragrance in honor of his first love, a woman he met in England, and gave it the nickname of his adored nephew Jacques. *Jicky* is enjoyed by both men and women, day and night.

Pictured Size: Photo courtesy of Guerlain, Inc.

L'Heure Bleue®
Launch Date: 1912

Fragrance Type: Perfume: Semi-Oriental, flowery. (Jacques Guerlain) The sensuality of *L'Heure Bleue* comes from a captivating mix of rose, jasmine, vanilla, and balsamic notes. This fragrance was inspired by the brief moment when the sky has lost the sun but not yet found the stars. A romantic interlude with nature, *L'Heure Bleue's* floral bouquet is tenderly warm and captivating; perfect for a woman of romance and distinction.

Bottle Design: Designed in the early part of the century at the height of the Oriental fashion movement, both *Mitsouko* and *L'Heure Bleue* bear the markings of Far East influence. The flacon label whirls with fanciful lettering typical of the period. The stopper, a nod to French culture, is carved in the shape of a Gendarme's hat.

Package Design: The wooden boxes are inlaid with an ivory motif in a design taken from the East, with mystical trees and birds.

Pictured Size: Photo courtesy of Guerlain, Inc.

127

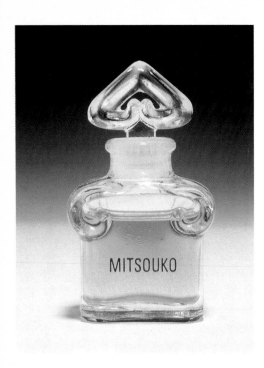

Mitsouko®

Launch Date: 1919

Fragrance Type: Perfume: Chypre, spicy and fruity. (Jacques Guerlain). *Mitsouko* is a masterpiece of harmony, composed of chypre, spices, hesperides, lilac, peach, oak moss, and vetiver. *Mitsouko*, a Japanese word meaning "mystery," was created for a woman with an introspective, intense and passionate nature. Inspired by character in Claude Farrère's novel, *The Battle*, a story about the ill-fated love of an Englishman and the wife of the ship's commander—a beautiful Japanese woman called Mitsouko - the fragrance of the same name is daring and mysterious.

Bottle Design: Designed in the early part of the century at the height of the Oriental fashion movement, both *Mitsouko* and *L'Heure Bleue* bear the markings of Far East influence. The flacon label whirls with fanciful lettering typical of the period. The stopper is carved in the shape of a Gendarme's hat.

Package Design: The wooden boxes are inlaid with an ivory motif in a design taken from the East, with mystical trees and birds.

Pictured Size: .07oz.

Dimensions: 1-1/2 " h x 1" w

CPG: $17.00

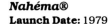

Nahéma®

Launch Date: 1979

Fragrance Type: Perfume: Floral, fruity, and woody. A kaleidoscope of floral and fruit notes, *Nahéma* is composed of rose, hyacinth, passion fruit, and exotic woods. *Nahéma* was inspired by Sheherazade's "One Thousand and One Nights," a tale of two princesses, alike in beauty, yet disparate in nature. One was gentle and warm, a wellspring of tenderness; the other was a woman of enigmatic intensity and deep unexplored passion. To reconcile this paradox, Jean-Paul Guerlain created *Nahéma*, meaning "daughter of fire."

Bottle Design: The flacon, in the Guerlain tradition, has contemporary lines with architectural inspiration. The body of the bottle is flat, the front slightly concave. The absolutely spherical stopper symbolizes the crystal ball that contains the secrets of the alchemist. The pearl-shaped drop encrusted in the body of the bottle evokes the quintessence of the perfume and the emotions it arouses.

Package Design: By Robert Granai. The outer package is matte and glossy black in color, with the familiar Guerlain zigzag pattern. The box is covered in black and gold, with a flower—

Nahéma—a flower of fire, in Bengali pink and orange shades. The bottle lies inside the box on a black and gold bed. The spray is decorated with a spray of flowers—Nahéma— inspired by the technique of oriental cloisonné work.
Pictured Size: Photo courtesy of Guerlain, Inc.

Parure®
Launch Date: 1975
Fragrance Type: Perfume: Chypre, flowery and fruity. (Jean-Paul Guerlain) This beautifully balanced and elegant perfume is a precious mix of oak moss, lilac, hesperides, plum, rose, patchouli, and spices. Like a cherished jewel, *Parure* was created for all women of taste who admire quality. Meaning "adornment" in the sense of a rare and flawless gem, Parure is all things precious and unique.
Bottle Design: Evoking an image of a turbulent sunset as the stopper emerges as a flame and open wings.
Package Design: By Robert Granai.
Pictured Size: Photo courtesy of Guerlain, Inc.
CPG: $12.00

Samsara®
Launch Date: 1989
Fragrance Type: Perfume: Floral, Oriental with dominant notes of sandalwood, ylang-ylang, jasmine, rose, narcissus, and balsamic notes. *Samsara* was created when Jean-Paul Guerlain encountered a woman so serene and sensual, so confident and feminine, that he wanted to capture her aura in a fragrance. A celebration of women's inner beauty, *Samsara* is a harmonious blend that explores serenity and seduction.
Bottle Design: Red bottle based on Tibetan figure in the Guimet Museum in Paris. Yellow bottle cap represents deep closed eyes. Commonly, many Buddhist statues can be found with the eyes closed.
Package Design: By Robert Granai.
Pictured Size: .07oz.
Dimensions: 1-1/2" h x 1-1/2" w
CPG: $12.00

Shalimar®
Launch Date: 1925
Fragrance Type: Perfume: Oriental. (Jacques Guerlain). This Oriental, woody, spicy fragrance is composed of hesperides, vanilla, jasmine, rose, and iris. Shalimar was inspired by the legendary love of an Indian emperor for his cherished wife—Mumtaz Mahal, the woman for whom the Taj Mahal was built. The gardens in which their love grew were called the gardens of Shalimar. This perfume of temptation is warm, sensual, and provocative.
Bottle Design: The perfume flacon, designed by Raymond Guerlain and Baccarat, is also inspired by these gardens: its shape is reminiscent of a fountain in the garden and the cornflower blue sapphire stopper is symbolic of the water's flow.
Package Design: By Raymond Guerlain.
Pictured Size: .07oz.
Dimensions: 1" h x 1-1/8" w
CPG: $15.00

Vetiver®
Launch Date: 1959
Fragrance Type: Eau de Cologne: (Jean-Paul Guerlain). Woody and spicy Vetiver's dominant notes are spices, tobacco, tonka beans, and vetiver The base (and name) of this fragrance is an ingredient that is pressed from the roots of grass grown in India. A clean, herbaceous, sporty scent, Vetiver elevates man to a new plane where he can fold the world into his own dreams.
Package Design: By Raymond Guerlain.
Pictured Size: Photo courtesy of Guerlain, Inc.
CPG: $8.00

Vol de Nuit®

Launch Date: 1933

Fragrance Type: Perfume: (Jean-Paul Guerlain). Oriental, woody, and spicy. Designed to capture the spirit of uncertainty and excitement found in an adventure novel written by Antoine de Saint-Exupery, *Vol de Nuit*, or *"Night Flight,"* evokes daring passion and dauntless exploits.

Bottle Design: The bottle, a slim square of smoky glass, is etched in a golden sunburst radiating from the letters of its name. Evocative of an airplane propeller, the flacon recalls the glamour of that adventurous era of early aviation.

Package Design: By Raymond Guerlain.

Pictured Size: Photo courtesy of Guerlain, Inc.

Other Guerlain Fragrances

Derby®

Launch Date: 1985

Fragrance Type: (Jean-Paul Guerlain). Woody, leathery and spicy. *Derby* is a harmonious mix of leather, spice, and patchouli and tobacco. The *Derby* man asserts his determination and strength through an unerring sense of elegance and refinement. He is wonderfully wild yet eminently civilized.

Bottle Design: Inspired by the Eagle of Nice as well as Japanese armor. The eagle became a warrior and the traces of the bird's open wings were inscribed little by little while the eagle's head and beak gave the stopper an aggressive but noble appearance. p. 150, Guerlain

Liu®

Launch Date: 1929

Fragrance Type: Floral, aldehyde. (Jacques Guerlain). Dominant notes are hesperides, jasmine, rose, and orange blossom. It was Pucini's last and greatest opera, Turandot, set in China, which inspired Jacques Guerlain to create *Liu*. Liu was the name of the beautiful young servant who gave her life to save her beloved, the unknown Prince, from death. Guerlain's *Liu* was inspired by this woman of tenderness and passion; a woman who gives generously of herself. *Liu* is a delicate and romantic fragrance, for a woman who is tender and confident, sentimental and passionate.

Bottle Design: *LIU* perfume in its black Baccarat flacon has not been sold for many years. The elegant bottle, designed by Raymond Guerlain, is reminiscent of the simple linearity of a Chinese black lacquer tea caddy. The prized tea from China was considered extremely valuable at the time of the creation of *LIU*, and the perfume bottle in this presentation alludes to the precious contents held within. The perfume name, etched elegantly in gold, bears the influence of art deco design.

Mouchoir de Monsieur®

Launch Date: 1904

Fragrance Type: (Jacques Guerlain). Citrus and aromatic, *Mouchoir de Monsieur* is a bouquet of citrus, hesperides, lavender, iris, woody accord and floral accent. The year is 1904: opulence and extravagance are the order of the day. It is a time of elegant dinners in honor of dukes and duchesses, princes and princesses. Throughout Paris, the energy of the new century explodes, and *Mouchoir de Monsieur*, with its fresh aromatic scent and woody base, perfectly capture the spirit of the era.

Bottle Design: *Mouchoir de Monsieur*, or "Gentleman's Handkerchief," was one of the first representational bottles. Its bottle has a triangular section and on each of its three sides, it bears a molded spiral motif, with a matching stopper and three-sided box. Because of its spiral design, it is referred to internally as the "snail" bottle.

guerlain
PARIS

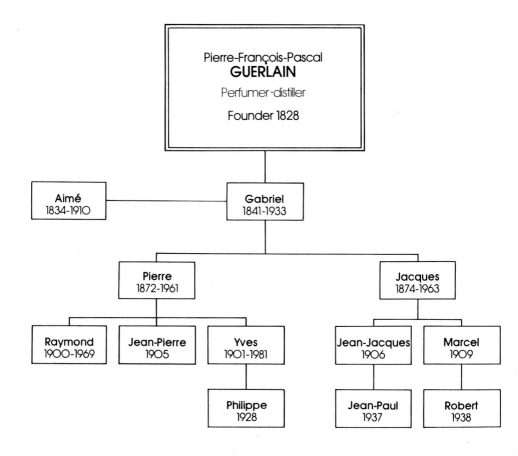

Pierre-François-Pascal
GUERLAIN
Perfumer-distiller
Founder 1828

Aimé
1834-1910

Gabriel
1841-1933

Pierre
1872-1961

Jacques
1874-1963

Raymond
1900-1969

Jean-Pierre
1905

Yves
1901-1981

Jean-Jacques
1906

Marcel
1909

Philippe
1928

Jean-Paul
1937

Robert
1938

Guy Laroche
Guy Laroche Paris

Drakkar Noir®
Launch Date: 1982
Fragrance Type: Eau de Toilette: Spicy, mossy, and woody.
Pictured Size: .17oz.
Dimensions: 2" h x 1" w
CPG: $7.00

Fidji®
Launch Date: 1966
Fragrance Type: Perfume: Fresh top notes are blended with light floral middle notes. Base notes are powdery.
Pictured Size: .06oz.
Dimensions: 1-1/8" h x 1" w
CPG: $5.00

Fidji®
Launch Date: 1966
Fragrance Type: Eau de Toillete
Pictured Size: .16oz.
Dimensions: 1-3/4" h x 1" w
CPG: $8.00

Horizon® Pour Homme
Launch Date: 1994
Fragrance Type: Eau de Toilette: Fresh, woody, and spicy.
Bottle Design: Iceberg glass bottle in "chiseled" rock-like fashion.
Pictured Size: .17oz.
Dimensions: 1-3/4" h x 1" w
CPG: $9.00

Other Guy Laroche Fragrances

Drakkar®
Launch Date: 1972

J'ai Osé®
Launch Date: 1977
Fragrance Type: This floral-oriental mixture reveals top notes that are fruity and spicy. Heart notes that are woody and floral mingle with warm, balsamic base notes.

H. ALPERT
H. Alpert & Co. Inc.

Listen®
Launch Date: 1989
Fragrance Type: Parfum: Floral-Fruity.
Pictured Size: .125oz.
Dimensions: 2" h x 1-1/2" w
CPG: $8.00

Other H. Alpert Fragrances

Listen® for Men
Launch Date: 1991
Fragrance Type: Chypre

HALSTON

Catalyst®
Launch Date: 1993
Fragrance Type: Parfum: Top notes include
jonquil, tuberose, otto of rose, and jasmine
absolute. At the heart, notes of muguet, cassias,
and violet are blended with patchouli, sandalwood,
musk, oakmoss, and vetiver to create the base
notes.
Bottle Design: Flared skirt design.
Pictured Size: .12oz.
Dimensions: 2-1/2 " x1" w
CPG: $10.00

Catalyst® *For Men*
Launch Date: 1994
Fragrance Type: Eau de Toilette: Woody-Spicy:
Top notes of lavender, sage, mint, and citrus blend
with spicy middle notes of clove, nutmeg, and
cinnamon. Base notes are sandalwood, oakmoss,
musk, amber, labdanum.
Bottle Design: Lab beaker.
Pictured Size: .25oz.
Dimensions: 2-1/4 " x 1-3/8" w
CPG: $6.00

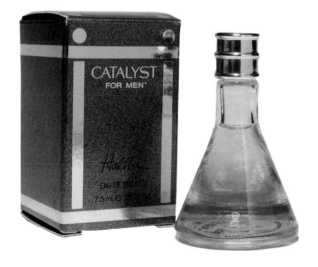

Halston Couture®
Launch Date: 1975 (U.S.A.)
Fragrance Type: Parfum: Fresh green florals, citrusy and fruity top notes. Floral middle notes are carnation, jasmine, and marigold. Base notes are sandalwood, patchouli, and animal notes.
Pictured Size: .125oz.
Dimensions: 2-1/8 " x 1" w
CPG: $9.00

Halston 101®
Launch Date: 1984
Fragrance Type: Cologne
Pictured Size: .125oz.
Dimensions: 2-1/8 " x 1-1/8" w
CPG: $8.00

Halston Z-14®
Launch Date: 1976
Fragrance Type: Cologne for Men: Chypre, leathery, spicy, and refined.
Pictured Size: .25oz.
Dimensions: 2 " x 1-1/2" w
CPG: $7.00

Other Halston Fragrances

Halston Night®
Launch Date: 1980
Fragrance Type: Leafy greens and fruity notes lead the way to elegant floral middle notes. Base notes are powdery and sensual.

Halston 1-12®
Launch Date: 1976
Fragrance Type: Chypre

Nautica®
Launch Date: 1992
Fragrance Type: Cologne: Chypre: citrusy, woody fragrance.
Pictured Size: .5oz.
Dimensions: 3 " x 2" w
CPG: $7.00

HELENA RUBINSTEIN
Helena Rubinstein, Inc.

emotion®
Launch Date: c1960
Fragrance Type: Eau de Parfum
Pictured Size: .25oz.
Dimensions: 2" h x 1-1/8" w
CPG: $7.00

Other Helena Rubinstein Fragrances

Courant®
Launch Date: 1972
Fragrance Type: Top notes are spicy and citrusy while the heart notes are precious florals. Base notes are sweet, ambered, and woody.

Heaven Scent®
Launch Date: 1941
Fragrance Type: Eau de Parfum

Heaven Scent Vanilla®
Launch Date: 1994
Fragrance Type: Eau de Parfum

Fun Facts
on Clary Sage
Clary sage is said to improve the memory and "quicken the senses."

HELENE CURTIS

Magic Secret®
Launch Date: c1960
Fragrance Type: Perfume
Pictured Size: .20oz.
Dimensions: 2 -3/4" h x 3/4" w
CPG: $3.00

HOLZMAN & STEPHANIE
Esther Holzman & Stephanie Holzman
Holzman & Stephanie Perfumes, Ltd.

Holzman & Stephanie's Fascination™
Launch Date: 1990
Fragrance Type: Perfume: Return to the age of refinement, elegance, and romance with white flowers and just a touch of rare Chinese Osmanthus weaving throughout the fragrance while subtle musk notes and precious woods add depth and richness. Let an unforgettable love unfold.
Bottle Design: Pochet of France.
Package Design: Box is printed in black and gold.
Pictured Size: .25oz.
Dimensions: 2-1/2" h x 3/4" w
CPG: $65.00

Je T'Aime™
(I Love You)
Launch Date: 1988/89
Fragrance Type: Perfume: A floriental perfume that was two years in the making. All components are from the most expensive fragrance oils available worldwide—Bulgarian rose, mimosa, jasmine de Grasse, clove, tuberose, opopanax, vanilla. This fragrance is unsurpassed in its beauty—a most sensuous fragrance.
Bottle Design: Pochet of France.
Package Design: Box is printed in purple and gold.
Pictured Size: .25oz.
Dimensions: 2" h x 1" w
CPG: $55.00

La Parisienne™
Launch Date: 1989
Fragrance Type: Perfume: Light floral, this fragrance was brilliantly conceived on the estate of the Holzman family with its many Linden trees. Bulgarian rose, jasmine, linden, and lily of the valley makeup the main components of this exciting and elegant scent.
Bottle Design: Pochet of France.
Package Design: Box is printed in pink and gold.
Pictured Size: .25oz.
Dimensions: 2-3/4" h x 1-1/4" w
CPG: $55.00

Fun Facts
on Misuki™
"Featured in the film *Scent of a Woman* with Al Pacino."
Holzman & Stephanie, 1994

Misuki™
Launch Date: 1987
Fragrance Type: Perfume: A classic oriental. A luscious blend of rosewood, lemon, peach, orchid, amber, and vanilla.
Bottle Design: Pochet of France.
Package Design: Swans, the symbol of longevity, grace this red and gold fragrance box.
Pictured Size: .25oz.
Dimensions: 2-1/4" h x 1-3/4" w
CPG: $65.00

HOUBIGANT
Jean-Francois Houbigant
Parfums Houbigant, Paris

Chantilly®
Launch Date: 1941
Fragrance Type: Perfume: Fresh, fruity top notes lead to heart notes that are spicy and floral. Base notes are sweet, balsamic, and powdery.
Pictured Size: .17oz.
Dimensions: 2-1/8" h x 1" w
CPG: $6.00

Ciao®
Launch Date: 1980
Fragrance Type: Parfum: This floral-chypre fragrance is rich with spicy and fruity top notes mingled with sweet, floral heart notes. Base notes are warm, powdery, and mossy.
Pictured Size: .25oz.
Dimensions: 3" h x 1-3/8" w
CPG: $16.00

Fun Facts
on Jean-François Houbigant
Established in 1775, The House of Houbigant served as perfumer
to such royalty as Queen Victoria and the Tsar of Russia.

140

Demi-Jour®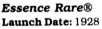
Launch Date: 1988
Fragrance Type: Parfum: Floral
Pictured Size: .125oz.
Dimensions: 1-1/2" h x 1" w
CPG: $6.00

Essence Rare®
Launch Date: 1928
Fragrance Type: Perfume: Delightfully cool green notes start this aromatic journey to the heart of radiant florals. Base notes are sensual and woody.
Bottle Design: Iceberg bottle and stopper.
Pictured Size: .25oz.
Dimensions: 1-3/4" h x 1" w
CPG: $20.00 - $25.00

Lutèce®
Launch Date: 1984
Fragrance Type: Parfum: Floral
Pictured Size: .12oz.
Dimensions: 2" h x 1-3/8" w
CPG: $6.00

Présence®
Launch Date: 1984
Fragrance Type: Parfum: Floral, woody, and spicy.
Pictured Size: .12oz.
Dimensions: 2" h x 1-1/4" w
CPG: $6.00

Quelques Fleurs®
Launch Date: 1912
Fragrance Type: Parfum: Florals: Green notes and citrus oils are blended with floral middle notes. Floral base notes are sweet and powdery.
Bottle Design: Redesigned in 1985. Glass bottle and stopper are created with a stylish flower petal design.
Package Design: Re-packaged in 1985.
Pictured Size: .10oz.
Dimensions: 1-1/4" h x 1-1/4" w
CPG: $10.00

Raffinée®
(Refined or delicate)
Launch Date: 1982
Fragrance Type: Parfum: Fruity, floral top notes flow into exotic floral middle notes. Base notes are sweet, spicy, and powdery.
Package Design: Lacquered red and gold.
Pictured Size: .125oz.
Dimensions: 2-1/8" h x1" w
CPG: $7.00

Other Houbigant Fragrances

Etude®
Launch Date: 1931

Ideal®
Launch Date: 1900

Les Fleurs®
Launch Date: 1983
Fragrance Type: Floral: Top notes are fresh and flowery. Middle notes are light, fresh florals blended with powdery base notes.

ICEBERG

Iceberg Parfum®
Launch Date: 1989
Fragrance Type: Parfum: Floral-Fruity: A blend of narcissus, lily of the valley, and violets that is warmed with notes of jasmine and geranium.
Pictured Size: .17oz.
Dimensions: 1-3/4" h x 2" w
CPG: $6.00

Other Iceberg Fragrances

Iceberg® Homme
Launch Date: 1991
Fragrance Type: A light touch of fern and sparkling fresh essences of lemon, orange flowers, and bergamot blended with hints of geranium, mossy, woody, musk, and vetiver elements.

Twice Iceberg®
Launch Date: 1995
Fragrance Type: Hints of lily of the valley, melon, and peach with a bouquet of violet, rose, and gardenia and a blend of musk, amber, and honey.

Issey Miyaké

L'Eau D'Issey®
Launch Date: 1992
Fragrance Type: Parfum: Elegant floral fragrance.
Pictured Size: .10oz.
Dimensions: 3" h x 3/4" w
CPG: $22.50 (1994 Collection Set)

Other Issey Miyaké Fragrances

L'Eau D'Issey® Pour Homme
Launch Date: 1995

Fun Facts
Fragrance at Work
Sprinkles of fragrant mists loom in the air of Japanese factories and offices;
keeping workers alert and increasing productivity.

J. Del Pozo

Duende®
Launch Date: 1994
Fragrance Type: Parfum: Floral-Woody: Bergamot,
linden, melon, and mandarin are the top noes with
jasmine and mimosa at the heart. Base notes are
sandalwood, cedar, thyme, and mugwort.
Pictured Size: .17oz.
Dimensions: 3-1/2" h x 1-1/4" w
CPG: $11.00

Other J. del Pozo Fragrances

Quasar®
Launch Date: 1995
Fragrance Type: Eau de Toilette

Fun Facts
Duende®
In the Castillion Spanish dialect, *Duende* means ghost or spirit of a woman.

J. Marc Sinan
Parfums J. Marc Sinan - Paris

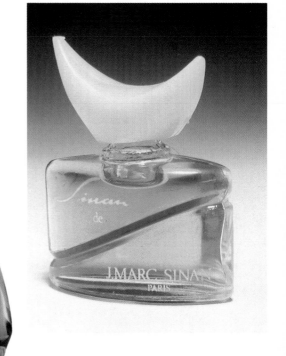

Sinan®
Launch Date: 1981 (Reintroduced 1990)
Fragrance Type: Perfume: Chypre-Floral.
Pictured Size: .06oz.
Dimensions: 1-1/2" h x 1-1/8" w
CPG: $9.00

Jaclyn Smith
Max Factor & Co.

California®
Launch Date: 1989
Fragrance Type: Eau de Cologne
Pictured Size: .10oz.
Dimensions: 2" h x 1-1/4" w
CPG: $5.00

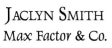

California® for Men
Launch Date: 1990
Fragrance Type: Cologne
Pictured Size: .10oz.
Dimensions: 2-1/8" h x 1" w
CPG: $4.00

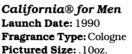

JACQUES BOGART
Parfums Jacques Bogart Paris

Witness®
"A new vision of the world"
Launch Date: 1992
Fragrance Type: Eau de Toilette: The initial fragrance of Witness is radiantly fresh, with head notes of Californian lemon and mandarin orange, punctuated by a fruity blend of grapefruit and pineapple, with slightly green notes thanks to the presence of galbanum from Iran. The whole is enveloped by rustic notes of lavender, rosemary, and aromatic artemesia. Then the originality of the fragrance floats up warm and strong thanks to its heart notes—richly blended spices, nutmeg, pimento, cinnamon, and clove. This is supported and developed by notes of juniper, thyme, cardamom, cinnamon leaf, and cumin. This powerful bend of long-lasting and pervasive spices lingers, leaving the scent of the body notes, a triple combination: (woody-ambergris, patchouli, plum-tree evernia, citrus), softened by a resin complex (benzoin, myrrh, opopanax) and fixed by leather and animal scents.
Bottle Design: The bottle has been designed by Joel Degrippes.
Package Design: The package is designed to evoke, by means of its materials, certain documents whose patina is witness to their long journey through time. Palimpsest, parchment, medieval illuminations, and an occult sign reflect the charm of writing materials used by humankind throughout the ages to bear witness and communicate.

Eau Fresh®
Launch Date: Undetermined
Fragrance Type: Eau de Toilette: Eau Fresh aims at being a pure, light, and pleasant freshness which does not overlook the personality. Its color recall waters rising in mountain lakes, both icy and transparent, wherein strength is born of the encounter amongst vital fluxes, at the heart of a preserved nature. This refreshing toilet water is distinguished by a lively and dazzling top note. The notes of mandarin, bergamot, and lemon follow the orange effects of Tunisian neroli and Para-guayan "Petit Grain." A tonic aspect, due to the green anise harmony of galbanum, caraway, and tarragon, is punctuated by a zesty fruit note of pineapple and grapefruit. Preceding and introduc-ing the middle note, rosemary and lavandin purif the aromatic form. The flowery heart of geranium jasmine, and lily of the valley is enhanced by light notes of coriander and nutmeg. This olfactive dominant of top-middle notes is followed by an accompaniment of bottom woody notes: Java vetiver, Indonesian patchouli, oak moss, and pine needle scents. Finally, the musks provide a certai softness to the overall effect.
Bottle Design: The Eau Fresh bottle has a structured and powerful shape, a pure and classical architecture. The material in a "frosted" glass and the frost green color immediately evoke a fresh and natural universe.
Package Design: Its modern packaging, with its recycled cardboard look, honeycombed all aroun in "pastel" notes, is pleasant to the touch.

Fun Facts
On Jacques Bogart
"From its origins, Jacques Bogart has claimed the exclusive territory of the male: "Bogart creates only for men."
Fragrance Marketing Group, 1995

Furyo®
Launch Date: 1988
Fragrance Type: Fougère - Woody and ambered.

One Man Show®
Launch Date: 1980
Fragrance Type: Chypre-Leathery.

JACQUES FAITH

Fath de Fath®
Launch Date: Undetermined
Fragrance Type: Eau de Toilette: Fruity, floral notes blended with woody notes.
Pictured Size: .17oz.
Dimensions: 1-1/2" h x 3/4" w
CPG: $22.00 (Gift set)

JALAND
Jaland Parfums, NYC

Twinkle®
Launch Date: 1930s
Pictured Size: .375oz.
Dimensions: 2" h x 1-3/4" w
CPG: $4.00

JAMES A. GALANOS
Parfums Galanos

Galanos®
Launch Date: 1979 (Reintroduced Fall, 1995)
Fragrance Type: Parfum: Oriental: Among several top notes are lemon, orange, mandarin, and chamomile with a floral heart of orange flower, jasmine, ylang-ylang, muguet, and carnations. Base notes include musk, amber, vetiver, cedarwood, sandalwood, and patchouli.
Pictured Size: .25oz.
Dimensions: 2 " h x 1-3/4" w
CPG: $4.00

> **Fun Facts**
> on James A. Galanos
> American fashion designer.

JEAN D'ALBRET

Écusson®
Launch Date: 1952
Fragrance Type: Parfum: Classic floral.
Pictured Size: .10oz.
Dimensions: 1-1/2" h x 1" w
CPG: $12.00 - $15.00

JEAN DESPREZ
Groupe Inter Parfums

Bal á Versailles®
Launch Date: 1962
Fragrance Type: Eau de Toilette: The rigor and the classicism of the bottle contains the nobility of this perfume, which is composed of natural essences. Top notes contain jasmine, rose, orange flower, and cassie farnese. At the heart is patchouli, santal, and vetiver. Base notes are civet and amber.
Bottle Design: Majestic in the roundness, the bottle of *Bal á Versailles* evokes the favorable period when France was radiant.
Pictured Size: .17oz.
Dimensions: 2-1/8" h x 1-3/8" w
CPG: $5.00

Fun Facts
Bal a Versailles®
"Born of the imagination of sculptor Leon Leyritz and the inspiration of Jean Desprez, this collection consists of 10 minatures, painted after the designs of Fragonard."
Groupe Inter Parfums

Escarmouche®
Launch Date: 1950
Fragrance Type: Perfume
Pictured Size: .06oz.
Dimensions: 1-1/8" h x 3/4" w
CPG: $5.00

148

Other Jean Desprez Fragrances

Crêpe ole Chine®
Launch Date: 1928
Fragrance Type: Chypre

Etourdissant®
Launch Date: 1950
Fragrance Type: Classic chypre

Grande Dame®
(Great Lady)
Launch Date: 1939
Fragrance Type: Flowery-Oriental.

Jardanel®
Launch Date: 1938

Revolution a Versailles®
Launch Date: 1989

Sheherazade®
Launch Date: 1983
Fragrance Type: Fruity, floral notes with spicy, woody notes.

Versailles® pour Homme
Launch Date: 1980
Fragrance Type: Floral top notes combine with mossy notes, and rare spices.

Votre Main®
(Your Hand)
Launch Date: 1938

JEAN PATOU
Jean Patou, Inc.

> **Fun Facts**
> 1000®
> "When first launched in 1972, a three gram sample was delivered by chauffeured Rolls Royce to the one hundred most elegant women in Paris."
> Jean Patou, Inc.

1000®
Launch Date: 1972
Fragrance Type: Eau de Toilette: Rare essential oils blended with enhanced floral notes and a sensual, woody note of mysor santal (Indian tree).
Pictured Size: .07oz.
Dimensions: 1-3/8" h x 1" w
CPG: $8.00

JOY®
"Joy to the World"
Launch Date: 1931
Fragrance Type: Eau de Toilette: Essential oils of
florals, florals, and more florals. Approximately
100 oils and essences are blended to perfection for
this "addictive scent."
Pictured Size: .07oz.
Dimensions: 1-3/8" h x 1" w
CPG: $8.00

Sublime®
"an instant of sheer happiness"
Launch Date: 1991
Fragrance Type: Eau de Parfum: Intoxicating mix
of pure flowers, warm amber musks, and muted
notes.
Bottle Design: Suspended in an exquisite bottle,
sculptured to fit a woman's hand, and capped with
a golden stopper shaped like a bud on the verge of
blossoming.
Package Design: A yellow and gold box, glorious
as the sun itself.
Pictured Size: .14oz.
Dimensions: 1-3/4" h x 1" w
CPG: $10.00

Other Jean Patou Fragrances

Câline®
Launch Date: 1964
Fragrance Type: Fresh and dry green and spicy notes are the top notes. Middle notes are classic florals that are blended with woody, mossy base notes.

Moment Suprême®
Launch Date: 1929
Fragrance Type: Eau de Toilette: Head and heart notes: This classic floral fragrance is fresh and enhanced with mossy, balsamic base notes.

JEAN-CHARLES BROSSEAU
Groupe Inter Parfums

> **Fun Facts**
> Jean-Charles Brosseau
> "A brief apprenticeship with Jacques Fath was all the introduction he needed to fashion, he created his own line at the age 24. Escaping from haute couture to ready-to-wear, Jean-Charles Brosseau hats and accessories are the toast of fashion press."
> Group Inter Parfums

Ombre D'Or®
Launch Date: 1994
Fragrance Type: Parfum: Conceived by Jean-Charles Brosseau, "a perfume dreamed like liquid light," and created by Nathalie Lorson and Martine Pallix (International Flavors & Fragrances). At dawn, bergamot and hyacinth awaken in the freshness of lily-of-the-valley and cyclamen to

mingle with the acidulated fragrances of tangerine and orange blossom. At noon, dainty peonies blush deep red in the languorous scent of acacias, freesias, and ylang-ylang. Scarlet rose sweetens it with its timeless fragrance while violet and jasmine are passionately entwined. A tender, subtle floral harmony spiced with glints of heather, vivacious gilly flower, and downy peach. In the twilight, deeper scents emerge: sandalwood unfolds its sensual fragrance in a natural blend both vetiver and cedar. Lastly, suave accents of vanilla nestle in the golden warmth of amber and musks to instill the gathering night with deep oriental mystery.

Bottle Design: A thick, flat form of glass, simply engraved with a bouquet of flowers held with a ribbon. Bare of any inscription, the flask confirms its creator's intention to identify and claim his work without resorting to signing it. The bottle itself is a charming object, an amulet to be saved and treasured. The glass is of such superb quality that the etched designs it bears takes on an imposing relief, veiling the liquid inside with gold, while allowing gleams of brilliance to sparkle through the transparent spaces.

Package Design: The gift box further embodies the brand of modern classicism. Fine Ingres cardboard excites the eye with the purity of a nearly ivory-colored white; the splendor of old gold crowns the creation with the house's floral emblem.

Pictured Size: .13oz.
Dimensions: 2" h x 1-1/4" w
CPG: $8.00

Ombre Rose®

Launch Date: 1981 (1982 U.S.A.)
Fragrance Type: Parfum: Created by Jean-Charles Brosseau. A "very French" floral-oriental. Its initial flowery, sweet notes of iris, lily of the valley, ylang-ylang, and honey, give way to the suave warmth of peach, sandalwood and musk. The first whiff of the powdery, sensual combination immediately charms with its subtle presence.

Bottle Design: Ombre Rose is packaged in Art Deco bottles decorated with a design of oriental inspiration (floral motif).

Package Design: White box with raised floral motif.

Pictured Size: .16oz.
Dimensions: 2" h x 1-1/2" w
CPG: $7.00

JEAN PAUL GAULTIER

Jean Paul Gaultier®
Launch Date: Fall, 1994
Fragrance Type: Eau de Parfum: Oriental florals with the hints of woody notes.
Bottle Design: Torso figure in frosted glass bottle.
Pictured Size: .10oz.
Dimensions: 2-1/4" h x1" w
CPG: $22.50 • (1994 Holiday Jewels Fragrance Collection Set)

JEAN-LOUIS SCHERRER
Parfums Jean-Louis Scherrer

Scherrer®
Launch Date: 1979
Fragrance Type: Eau de Parfum: Fruity and floral notes are blended with woody, mossy, and powdery base notes.
Pictured Size: .125oz.
Dimensions: 2-3/4" h x1" w
CPG: $7.00

> **Fun Facts**
> on Jean-Louis Scherrer
> Studied classical ballet at the Pairs Conservatory.

> **Fun Facts**
> on Nuits Indiennes®
> Inspired by Gustav Klimt painting, *"The Kiss."*

Nuits Indiennes®
Launch Date: 1993
Fragrance Type: Eau de Parfum: Oriental: Spicy and ambered.
Pictured Size: .12oz.
Dimensions: 3" h x3/4" w
CPG: $8.00

Other Scherrer Fragrances

Scherrer 2®
Launch Date: 1986
Fragrance Type: Floral-Aldehydic.

JIL SANDER
Jil Sander Wiesbaden

Jil Sander No 4®
Launch Date: 1990
Fragrance Type: Eau de Parfum: Floral
Pictured Size: .17oz.
Dimensions: 1-1/2" h x 1" w
CPG: $7.00

Other Jil Sander Fragrances

Jil Sander®
Launch Date: 1981
Fragrance Type: Eau de Parfum: Top notes are spicy and leafy green. Middle notes are florals with warm, balsamic, mossy base notes.

Woman two®
Launch Date: 1983
Fragrance Type: Perfume: Fruity top notes with exotic floral heart notes. Base notes are sensual and woody accords.

JITROIS
J.C. Jitrois

Jitrois®
Launch Date: 1989
Fragrance Type: Parfum: Chypre-Floral.
Pictured Size: .17oz.
Dimensions: 2" h x 1-1/2" w
CPG: $11.00

JOAN COLLINS
Parlux Fragrances, Inc.

Spectacular®
Launch Date: 1989
Fragrance Type: Perfume: Floral
Pictured Size: .17oz.
Dimensions: 2-1/2" h x 1-3/8" w
CPG: S8.00

JOOP!
Wolfgang Joop Parfums JOOP!, Paris

Joop! ® Parfum pour Femme
Launch Date: 1993
Fragrance Type: Eau de Toilette Femme: Floral
and fruity notes. Oriental blends add to this
unique fragrance.
Pictured Size: .10oz.
Dimensions: 1-3/4" h x 3/4" w
CPG: S7.00

Joop!® pour Homme
Launch Date: 1993
Fragrance Type: Eau de Toilette Homme: Spicy
and florals mixed with a woody background.
Pictured Size: .17oz.
Dimensions: 1-3/4" h x 1" w
CPG: S7.00

Berlin®
Launch Date: 1994 Undetermined
Fragrance Type: Eau de Toilette
Pictured Size: .17oz.
Dimensions: 2-1/2" h x 1-3/8" w
CPG: $8.00

Nightflight®
Launch Date: 1994 Undetermined
Fragrance Type: Eau de Toilette: Fruits and sandalwood.
Pictured Size: .17oz.
Dimensions: 2" h x 1" w
CPG: $6.00

JOVAN
Div. of Coty, Inc.

adidas®
Launch Date: 1986
Fragrance Type: Eau de Toilette: Leathered-Chypre. A virile blend of crisp, clean, citrusy and spicy top and middle notes blend with bold bottom notes of patchouli and woody notes combined with oakmoss and leather to add warmth and depth to this sportive creation.
Pictured Size: .23oz.
Dimensions: 2" h x 1" w
CPG: $3.00

Whisper of Musk®
Launch Date: 1984
Fragrance Type: Cologne: Woody and musky.
Pictured Size: .13oz.
Dimensions: 2" h x 1-1/8" w
CPG: $4.00

Other Jovan Fragrances

Ginseng® for Men
Launch Date: 1975
Fragrance Type: Herbaceous-Woody. (The Fragrance Foundation Reference Guide 1979)

Ginseng® for Women
Launch Date: 1975
Fragrance Type: Woody-Oriental. (The Fragrance Foundation Reference Guide 1979)

Jovan Andron® for Men
Launch Date: 1982
Fragrance Type: Woody, leathery, chypre.

Jovan Andron® for Women
Launch Date: 1982
Fragrance Type: Oriental-Ambered.

Jovan Island Gardenia®
Launch Date: 1982
Fragrance Type: Floral. A soft, sensuous breeze from the islands carries the scent of floral top notes. The balmy air releases the mysterious middle notes of a tropical rainforest with precious woods that are softened with sultry mosses.

Jovan Musk® For Women
Launch Date: 1972
Fragrance Type: Perfume: Aldehydic musk. Top notes are delicate aldehyde floral accords lightly blended with a bottom note of earthy musk.

Jovan Musk® For Men
Launch Date: 1973
Fragrance Type: Citrus Musk. Top notes are a masterpiece of lavender, lemon, and a touch of spearmint blended with exotic spicy, woody middle notes boldly supported by amber and musk base notes.

Jovan Musk Evening Edition®
Launch Date: 1985
Fragrance Type: Musk

Jovan Sex Appeal® for Men
Launch Date: 1975
Fragrance Type: Fougère: Spicy, ambered, and oriental. Brisk citrus top notes accent sexy middle notes of spice and rich woods blended with erotic base notes of amber and musk. (The Fragrance Foundation Reference Guide 1979)

Jovan Sex Appeal® for Women
Launch Date: 1976
Fragrance Type: Modern Oriental blend. (The Fragrance Foundation Reference Guide 1979)

Jovan VSP®
Launch Date: 1973
Fragrance Type: Modern Floral. (The Fragrance Foundation Reference Guide 1979) Top notes are fresh and spicy while middle notes are spicy and floral. Base notes are powdery and feminine.

Jovan White Musk® for Men
Launch Date: 1992
Fragrance Type: Fresh musk describes this fragrance. The fresh clean citrus top note, together with traces of spice create a warm amber, musk heart that is complimented by middles notes that are fruity with a sea-like freshness creating the fragrance signature. Base notes are ambered and musky.

Jovan White Musk® for Women
Launch Date: 1990
Fragrance Type: This alluring fragrance is a floral musk. Flashes of aldehydes and bergamot as the top notes are followed by floral and spicy middle notes. Base notes of musk, soft woods, and amber generate the warm, feminine fragrance.

Jovan Woman®
Launch Date: 1977
Fragrance Type: Spicy oriental. Floral top notes highlight this extraordinary bouquet. Middle notes of exotic spices accent the sultry, woody, and amber base notes.

Jungle Gardenia®
Launch Date: 1958
Fragrance Type: Sweet floral. Top notes are exotic florals enhanced by floral accords at the heart laced with sandalwood. Bottom notes are oakmoss and amber.

Lady®
Launch Date: 1983
Fragrance Type: Top notes are green notes blended with citrus and fruity notes. Middle notes are florals emphasizing rose. Base notes are balsamic and very sensual.

Lily of the Valley®
Launch Date: 1988
Fragrance Type: Green floral. A fresh-picked floral bouquet of top notes is complimented with a touch of floral middle notes. Base notes are floral and woody.

Madame Jovan®
Launch Date: 1975
Fragrance Type: Modern Floral. (The Fragrance Foundation Reference Guide 1979) Floral notes of gardenia blended with citrus oils and leafy greens flow into elegant floral middle notes. Base notes are sensual, feminine, and woody.

Night Blooming Jasmine®
Launch Date: 1979
Fragrance Type: Aldehydic floral. Top notes are citrusy and floral. Rich floral middle notes are supported by a warm complex of mossy, woody, and amber base notes.

Touche®
Launch Date: 1979
Fragrance Type: Top notes are fruity while middle notes are elegant florals. Base notes are sweet, sensual, and powdery.

JUDITH MULLER

Bat-Sheba®
Launch Date: 1967
Fragrance Type: Parfum Toilette: Fruity and floral notes lead to the heart of more florals. Base notes are warm, ambered, leathery, and mossy.
Pictured Size: .5oz.
Dimensions: 3-1/4" h x 1-1/2" w
CPG: $35.00

Other Judith Muller Fragrances

Judith®
Launch Date: 1975
Fragrance Type: Fresh, fruity top notes are blended with fresh, floral middle notes. Base notes are woody and mossy.

Shalom®
Launch Date: 1970
Fragrance Type: Fruity top notes blended with fruity, floral middle notes. Base notes are mossy and balsamic.

JULIO IGLESIAS

Only®
Launch Date: 1989
Fragrance Type: Eau de Toilette: For millions of women throughout the world, Julio Iglesias is more than a superlative music talent, he is a warm and caring sentimentalist. It is for these women that he created *Only*. Top notes are warm and tropical with middle notes of violet, jasmine, and rose. Base notes are romantic sandalwood and balsam.
Pictured Size: .34oz.
Dimensions: 1-1/2" h x 2-1/4" w
CPG: $9.00

Only® for Men
Launch Date: Undetermined
Fragrance Type: *Only for Men* was created for the masculine, international man. Top notes are citrus and fruit. Spicy, floral middle notes blend with base notes that are ambered, woody, and musky.
Pictured Size: Photo Courtesy of Fragrance Marketing Group
CPG: $8.00

Other Julio Iglesias Fragrances

Only CRAZY®
Launch Date: Undetermined
Fragrance Type: A floral aromatic, *Only CRAZY* will enhance a woman's passion and romance through this exciting and sensual fragrance. Top notes are green, fruity, floral and fresh. Middle notes are spicy and floral with powdery, vanilla, ambered sensual base notes.

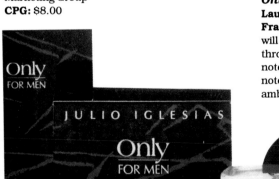

KANØN
Masson Agencies Ltð.

kanøn®
Launch Date: 1966
Fragrance Type: Cologne: A full-bodied fragrance—a complex blend of amber, spice, and musk. It's as fresh and invigorating as a clean mountain wind.
Pictured Size: Photo courtesy of Masson Agencies, Ltd.
Dimensions: 2-1/2" h x 1-1/4" w
CPG: $6.00 (.5oz.)

kanøn SPORT®
Launch Date: 1994
Fragrance Type: Eau de Toilette: A brisk aromatic/ozone complex consisting of sage, chamomile, cardamom, and basil, artfully blended with masculine notes of lavender and caraway. A vibrant accord of petit grain, bergamot, and rhubarb complete the top note. Middle note—a clean, spicy quality dominated by clove, cinnamon, and coriander round out the fragrance and is laced with a nuance of pineapple, lavender, and geranium. An adventurous touch of fruity cassis compliments the very complex woody accord of cedar, patchouli, sandalwood, and nutmeg. A rich undertone of musk, amber, labdanum, oakmoss, and a hint of leather complete this fragrances creation.
Package Design: In-house design at Massons.
Pictured Size: Photo courtesy of Masson Agencies, Ltd.
CPG: $8.00 (.5oz.)

KENZO
Kenzo Takada
Kenzo Paris Parfums

Kenzo®
Launch Date: 1988
Fragrance Type: Eau de Toilette: Floral:
Magnolia, gardenia, tuberose, vanilla, orange,
and peach.
Pictured Size: .125oz.
Dimensions: 1-1/8" h x 1-1/8" w
CPG: $8.00

Kenzo Parfum d'Été®
Launch Date: 1990
Fragrance Type: Eau de Toilette: Jasmine,
peony, rose, and green leaves.
Pictured Size: .17oz.
Dimensions: 2-1/2" h x 1-1/2" w
CPG: $11.00

Other Kenzo Fragrances

Kenzo® Pour Homme
Launch Date: 1991
Fragrance Type: Chypre: Woody and mossy.
Unlike most men's fragrances, *Kenzo Pour
Homme features* floral notes instead of citrus
notes.
Bottle Design: Frosted blue bottle gently
limbered like the bamboo shoot it emulates.
Packaging Design: Embossed bamboo motif.

KRIZIA
Parfums Krizia

K® de Krizia
Launch Date: 1979
Fragrance Type: Eau de Parfum: Leafy greens and spices create the top notes. Middle notes are elegant florals with sensual powdery base notes.
Pictured Size: .20oz.
Dimensions: 1-3/8" h x 1-1/8" w
CPG: $6.00

Fun Facts
on Krazy Krizia®
Awarded the 1992 Italian Academia del Profumo award.

Krazy Krizia®
Launch Date: 1992 (1993 U.S.A.)
Fragrance Type: Eau de Parfum: An oriental, fruity scent.
Bottle Design: A translucent, oval-shaped bottle. The gold tone top is designed to reflect the image of a panther's eye.
Pictured Size: .20oz.
Dimensions: 1-1/2" h x 1-3/8" w
CPG: $7.00

Moods® de Krizia
Launch Date: 1990
Fragrance Type: Eau de Parfum: Floral and spicy.
Pictured Size: .20oz.
Dimensions: 1-1/2" h x 1-3/4" w
CPG: $6.00

Teatro alla Scala®
Launch Date: 1986
Fragrance Type: Parfum: Floral
Pictured Size: .125oz.
Dimensions: 1-1/8" h x 1-3/4" w
CPG: $7.00

Other Krizia Fragrances

Krizia® Uomo
Launch Date: 1984
Fragrance Type: Chypre-Leathery.

Krazy® Uomo
Launch Date: 1993
Fragrance Type: Chypre-Leathery.

Moods® Uomo
Launch Date: 1989
Fragrance Type: Oriental-Woody.

> *Fun Facts*
> Dangerous Pleasures
> It is said that the tuberose represents "dangerous pleasures."

LA PERLA

La Perla®
Launch Date: 1987
Fragrance Type: Eau de Toilette: Chypre-Floral.
Pictured Size: .25oz.
Dimensions: 1-1/2" h x 2-1/2" w
CPG: $9.00

LAGERFELD
Karl Lagerfeld
Parfums Lagerfeld

Chloé®
Launch Date: 1975
Fragrance Type: Parfum: Fruity top notes with green accents blended into exotic floral middle notes with sensual, powdery, feminine base notes.
Bottle Design: Spherical glass bottle with calla lily stopper.
Pictured Size: .12oz.
Dimensions: 2-1/8" h x 1-1/8" w
CPG: $9.00

Chloé®
Launch Date: 1975
Fragrance Type: Parfum: Fruity top notes with green accents blended into exotic floral middle notes with sensual powdery feminine base notes
Bottle Design: Clear, hexagonal shaped.
Pictured Size: .17oz.
Dimensions: 1-1/2" h x 1-1/8" w
CPG: $5.00

Chloé Narcisse®
Launch Date: 1992
Fragrance Type: Parfum: Oriental

Bottle Design: Clear, hexagonal shaped.
Pictured Size: .17oz.
Dimensions: 1-1/2" h x 1-1/8" w
CPG: $5.00

164

Chloé Narcisse®
Launch Date: 1992
Fragrance Type: Parfum: Oriental
Pictured Size: .12oz.
Dimensions: 2-1/8" h x 1" w
CPG: $12.00

Lagerfeld®
Launch Date: 1979
Fragrance Type: Cologne: Oriental notes with woody, spicy, and tobacco notes.
Pictured Size: .17oz.
Dimensions: 2" h x 1" w
CPG: $7.00

Photo®
Launch Date: 1991
Fragrance Type: Cologne: Fougère-Fresh.
Pictured Size: .17oz.
Dimensions: 2" h x 1" w
CPG: $7.00

Other Lagerfeld Fragrances

KL®
Launch Date: 1982
Fragrance Type: Parfum: Spicy, oriental top notes mingle with spicy, floral middle notes and sweet, balsamic, ambered base notes.
Bottle Design: 1/2 sphere, spread fan, fashioned for Lagerfeld's love of fans.

Sun Moon Stars®
Launch Date: 1994
Fragrance Type: Parfum: Modern florals with fruity and oriental notes.
Bottle Design: Exquisitely sculptured replica of a planet with suns, moons and stars. Deep blue in color and topped with a spiraling gold tone stopper.

LALIQUE
Lalique Parfums

Lalique®
Launch Date: 1992
Fragrance Type: Eau de Toilette: Top notes are floral and fruity with gardenia, blackberry, and mandarin. The floral heart is of peony, magnolia, rose, ylang-ylang, and orange blossom. Base notes are sweet and woody with sandalwood, cedar, oakmoss, vanilla, musk, and amber.
Bottle Design: A transparent center is enfolded in a ring of sculpted leaves. Designed in the same leaf motif is the fan-shaped stopper.
Package Design: Colors are turquoise and terracotta.
Pictured Size: .15oz.
Dimensions: 2" h x 1-3/8" w
CPG: $13.00

LANCETTI

Lancetti®
Launch Date: 1976
Fragrance Type: Eau de Toilette: Floral
Pictured Size: .12oz.
Dimensions: 3-3/8" h x 1-1/8" w
CPG: $8.00

Lancôme
Armand Petitjean

Balafre®
Launch Date: 1967
Fragrance Type: Eau de Toilette: Oriental-Woody.
Pictured Size: .25oz.
Dimensions: 2" h x 1" w
CPG: $5.00

Magie Noire®
Launch Date: 1978
Fragrance Type: Perfume: Fruity and green notes
reveal the top notes while spicy, floral heart notes
compliment base notes that are woody, mossy, and
sensual.
Pictured Size: .25oz.
Dimensions: 2" h x 1-1/2" w
CPG: $10.00

Ô de Lancôme®
Launch Date: 1969
Fragrance Type: Eau de Toilette: Chypre: Fresh,
green notes.
Pictured Size: .25oz.
Dimensions: 2-1/2" h x 1-1/8" w
CPG: $7.00

Sagamore®

Launch Date: 1985
Fragrance Type: Eau de Toilette: A spicy-chypre with animal notes.
Bottle Design: Smoky gray bottle.
Pictured Size: .25oz.
Dimensions: 2" h x 1-1/8" w
CPG: $5.00

Sikkim®

Launch Date: 1971
Fragrance Type: Eau de Toilette: Top notes are herbaceous with floral middle notes. Base notes are warm, woody accords with a hint of leather.
Pictured Size: .125oz.
Dimensions: 2-3/8" h x 1/2" w
CPG: $5.00

Trésor®
Launch Date: 1950 (Reintroduced 1990)
Fragrance Type: Eau de Parfum: Floral
Pictured Size: .25oz.
Dimensions: 1-1/4" h x 1-1/2" w
CPG: $13.00

Trophèe®
Launch Date: 1982
Fragrance Type: Eau de Toilette: Chypre
Pictured Size: .125oz.
Dimensions: 1-3/4" h x 1-1/8" w
CPG: $5.00

Other Lancôme Fragrances

Cachet Bleu®
Launch Date: 1935

Climat®
Launch Date: 1967
Fragrance Type: A woody, classic floral, aldehyde fragrance.

Conquete®
Launch Date: 1935
Fragrance Type: Chypre with floral notes.

Fleches®
Launch Date: 1938

Gardenia®
Launch Date: 1937
Fragrance Type: Floral

Marrakech®
Launch Date: 1946

Peut-être®
(means perhaps, maybe)
Launch Date: 1937

Tropiques®
Launch Date: 1935
Fragrance Type: Spicy and aromatic.

LANVIN
Lanvin Parfums, Inc.
Jeanne Lanvin

Arpège®
Launch Date: 1927
Fragrance Type: Eau de Parfum: Floral-Aldehydic. Fruity and green notes to create top notes. Elegant floral heart notes lead to woody, powdery base notes.
Bottle Design: This bottle was introduced in 1995 and is a recreation of the 1927 formula.
Pictured Size: .25oz.
Dimensions: 1-3/4" h x 1-1/8" w
CPG: $22.00 (Gift set w/Box)

My Sin®
Launch Date: 1924
Fragrance Type: Parfum: Top notes are herbaceous with a fresh hint of citrus. Sweet, floral middle notes blend into sweet, balsamic, woody, base notes.
Pictured Size: .07oz.
Dimensions: 1-3/4" h x 1/2" w
CPG: $6.00

Rumeur®
Launch Date: 1934
Fragrance Type: Parfum
Pictured Size: .25oz.
Dimensions: 1-3/4" h x 3/4" w
CPG: $5.00

Other Lanvin Fragrances

Clair de Jour®
Launch Date: 1983
Fragrance Type: Fruity, floral scent.
Bottle Design: Lines emanate from around fragrance name symbolizing rays of sunlight around a glass bottle.

Scandal®
Launch Date: 1931
Fragrance Type: Herbaceous and citrusy top notes. Floral and leather middle notes lead the way for sweet, warm, and sensual base notes.

Via Lanvin®
Launch Date: 1971
Fragrance Type: Flowery top notes blend with floral heart notes and woody, powdery base notes.

Vetyver®
Launch Date: 1966
Fragrance Type: Citrusy: Vetiver, cedar, sandalwood, lemon, and orange.

LAPIDUS
Ted Lapidus
Parfums Ted Lapidus, Inc.

Création®
Launch Date: 1984
Fragrance Type: Parfum: Since the beginning of time, the meeting of sea and shore has evoked a loving, passionate and faithful embrace. In the surf, ardor and tenderness merge. The spirited forces of nature unite in mysterious harmony. At this mythical point lies CREATION, an exceptionally rich floral composition, a balanced symphony where the most subtle notes stand out. On opening the bottle, the head note springs out in a sumptuous bouquet of white flowers. The middle note contains a perfect blend of heady spices and luscious fruits. CREATION by TED LAPIDUS is a delicate yet powerful blend, a vibrant combination of rare scents. CREATION, an eternal homage to the woman of always, sensual and tender, passionate and affectionate.
Bottle Design: The ocean and the beach have left their mark on the bottle: stylized waves, frosted glass and a pebble-shaped top artfully and lovingly complete the work of CREATION.
Pictured Size: .14oz.
Dimensions: 2-1/8" h x 1-1/4" w
CPG: $5.00

Fantasme®
Launch Date: 1992

Fragrance Type: Parfum: An contribution to the new family of "soft oriental" fragrances. Very seductive, with an intimate pervasion which is never invasive. A bouquet of delicate flowers (rose, magnolia, freesia) and red fruits, over a warmer harmony of sandalwood and vanilla associated with modern musks.

Bottle Design: Both balanced with regard to its shape and very in its design, with the blue in relief forming an elegant bow knot.

Pictured Size: Photo Courtesy of Fragrance Marketing Group

CPG: $8.00

Lapidus® Pour Homme
Launch Date: 1987

Fragrance Type: Eau de Toilette: At the very heart of the masculine universe, *Lapidus Pour Homme* is light and spicy with lavender, bergamot, basil, petit-grain, thyme, mugwort, juniper, and coriander; rich and generous with frankincense, patchouli, and oak moss; real, sensual, and virile with amber, sandalwood, and musk. A harmonious alliance of force and elegance, of rigor and humor, of simplicity and seduction...in a moment of eternity.

Bottle Design: The bottle, created by Jacques Konckier, is a remarkable design and unites force and grace. Its gray opal, used for the first time in perfumery, has the magnificence and the solidity of marble.

Pictured Size: .14oz.

Dimensions: 2" h x 1" w

CPG: $4.00

Other Ted Lapidus Fragrances

Envol®
Launch Date: 1981

Fragrance Type: Fruity, green accords meet a heart of exotic florals. Base notes are woody, balsamic, and mossy.

VU®
Launch Date: 1976

Fragrance Type: Fruity, spicy top notes are blended with spicy, floral middle notes. Base notes are woody and mossy.

LAURA ASHLEY
Laura Ashley, Inc.

Dilys®
Launch Date: 1991
Fragrance Type: Eau de Parfum: Floral
Pictured Size: .17oz.
Dimensions: 1-3/4" h x 1-1/8" w
CPG: $7.00

Other Laura Ashley Fragrances

Laura Ashley No. 1®
Launch Date: 1989
Fragrance Type: Floral-Fruity.

LAURA BIAGIOTTI

Laura Biagiotti®
Launch Date: 1982
Fragrance Type: Parfum: Florals and greens create the tops notes while exotic florals accent heart notes that blend with mossy, powdery base notes.
Pictured Size: .17oz.
Dimensions: 2-3/8" h x 3/4" w
CPG: $6.00

Roma®
Launch Date: 1987
Fragrance Type: Perfume: This fragrance is warm and sensual with fresh, soft florals delicately balanced with slightly fruity notes. This scent is made without alcohol.
Bottle Design: Inspired by her love for the "eternal city." Ancient Rome column bottle design.
Pictured Size: .17oz.
Dimensions: 2"h x 1-1/8"w
CPG: $8.00

Venezia®
Launch Date: 1992
Fragrance Type: Eau de Toilette: Oriental-Ambered.
Bottle Design: Bottle design based on Harlequin figure in Italian literature.
Pictured Size: .17oz.
Dimensions: 2-1/2" h x 2" w
CPG: $12.00

Other Laura Biagiotti Fragrances

Venezia® Uomo
Launch Date: 1995

LENEL
Frances Rothschild
Lenel Perfumes, Inc.

Avante®
"For the woman who must play many roles"
Launch Date: Undetermined
Fragrance Type: Eau de Toilette: Created by Frances Rothschild. A light, refreshing fragrance with floral notes that add a touch of confidence to each part of your day.

Caressant®
Launch Date: c1950
Fragrance Type: Eau de Toilette: Velvety smooth blend in subtle proportions of mysterious Oriental essence complimented with floral notes fixed with luxurious musk from Asia.

Fun Facts
On Frances Rothschild
Frances Rothschild was awarded the MEDAIILE D'OR for her fragrance creations on three separate occasions—Paris, France 1979; Vienna, Austria, 1980-81; and Brussels 1982.

Dallas®
"The designer fragrance with a western flair"
Launch Date: Undetermined
Fragrance Type: Cologne: A long lasting fragrance of natural essences of citrus and herbs blended with woody under notes. A fresh outdoors fragrance that carries a man through the day with subtle earthy elegance and through the evening with sensuous warmth.

Lenel® for Men
Launch Date: Undetermined
Fragrance Type: Eau de Toilette: An elegant and sophisticated masculine fragrance of citrusy and herbaceous notes.

Private Affair®
Launch Date: 1979
Fragrance Type: Perfume: Pure sorcery concocted with French jasmine, Italian bergamot, gardenia, and muguet. The scent is accentuated and fixed for long qualities with priceless ambergris, and musk tonquin from Asia. This luxurious fragrance whispers of both sentiment and sophistication to make a woman seem precious and provocative at the same time.

Vestalia®
Launch Date: Undetermined
Fragrance Type: Parfum de Toilette: Pronounced Ves-TAHL-ya. The fragrance of fire, mystery and warmth. A chic blend of French and Oriental essence. Rose and jasmine from Italy and Asia.

Amber®
Launch Date: Undetermined
Fragrance Type: A woody, amber fragrance for the outdoor sportsman or sportswoman. This fragrance gives a fresh feeling of earthy woods and ferns.

Amber Rose®
Launch Date: Undetermined
Fragrance Type: A unique blend of floral notes for an essence of total femininity.

de Rothschild® for Men
"Love at first whiff"
Launch Date: Undetermined
Fragrance Type: Woody, green, and citrus blend of oriental essences that are fresh, crisp, and slightly spicy. Earthy woods and ferns give an outdoor feeling. Warm under notes of earthy, organic florals notes.

Exotic Musk Oil®
"The mythical scent casting a spell of Passion and Power..."
Launch Date: Undetermined
Fragrance Type: An earthy, natural fragrance of pure undiluted musk oil.

Strictly Personal®
Launch Date: 1979
Fragrance Type: A sophisticated blend of citron, herbs, and spices from Indonesia and South Africa. The spicy undertone helps make a teaser in so many exciting ways with bergamot from Italy, jasmine from Morocco, and orange blossoms from France.

Balahé®
Launch Date: 1987
Fragrance Type: Parfum Coffret: Fruity top notes blended with middle notes of exotic florals and sweet, woody, powdery base notes.
Pictured Size: .125oz.
Dimensions: 1-1/4" h x 1-1/4" w
CPG: $6.00

Léonard de Léonard®
Launch Date: 1989
Fragrance Type: Eau de Toilette: Floral-Green.
Pictured Size: .125oz.
Dimensions: 3" h x 3/4" w
CPG: $10.00

Tamango®
Launch Date: 1977
Fragrance Type: Eau de Toilette: Spicy oils and leafy greens lead the way to classic floral middle notes. Base notes are soft and powdery.
Package Design: Black lacquered case decorated with an orchid symbolizing fragrance.
Pictured Size: .125oz.
Dimensions: 1-1/2" h x 1-1/2" w
CPG: $5.00

Other Léonard Fragrances

Eau Fraiche®
Launch Date: 1974
Fragrance Type: Fruity and flowery with woody notes.

Fashion®
Launch Date: 1970
Fragrance Type: Fresh elegant floral.

Léonard® Pour Homme
Launch Date: 1979
Fragrance Type: Chypre-Leather.

LIZ CLAIBORNE
Liz Claiborne Cosmetics

Liz Claiborne®
Launch Date: 1986
Fragrance Type: Perfume: Floral-Fruity.
Pictured Size: .125oz.
Dimensions: 2" x 1-1/4"w
CPG: $11.00

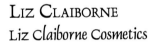

Realities®
Launch Date: 1990
Fragrance Type: Perfume: Floral
Pictured Size: .125oz.
Dimensions: 1-3/8" h x 1" w
CPG: $13.00

Vivid®
Launch Date: 1993
Fragrance Type: Parfum: Floral
Pictured Size: .125oz.
Dimensions: 1-3/4" h x 1" w
CPG: $11.00

LORENZO

Lorenzo® Pour Homme
Launch Date: Undetermined
Fragrance Type: Eau de Toilette
Pictured Size: .17oz.
Dimensions: 2" h x1-1/4" w
CPG: $4.00

LOUIS FÉRAUD
Avon Products, Inc.

Fantasque®
Launch Date: 1981
Fragrance Type: Parfum: Fruity top notes enhanced with vetiver and woody notes.
Pictured Size: .33oz.
Dimensions: 2-3/4" h x 1-3/4" w
CPG: $5.00

Other Louis Féraud Fragrances

Jour®
Launch Date: 1984
Fragrance Type: Fruity, floral scent.

LUCIANO SOPRANI
Luciano Soprani Profumi

Luciano Soprani®
Launch Date: 1987
Fragrance Type: Parfum: Oriental-Spicy.
Pictured Size: .17oz.
Dimensions: 1-3/8" h x 1-3/8" w
CPG: $8.00

Other Soprani Fragrances

Soprani® Uomo
Launch Date: 1988
Fragrance Type: Chypre-Leather.

MADLEINE MONO
Madeleine Mono, Ltd.

Madeleine de Madeleine®
Launch Date: 1980s
Fragrance Type: Parfum: An especially long
lasting and unique blend of rare French tuberose
absolute, Moroccan jonquil absolute, and French
mimosa absolute give the scent its highly indi-
vidual top note. Precious Turkish otto of rose and
French jasmine absolute combine with Roman
chamomile oil to give the fragrance its very rich
and sensuous middle notes. The latter blends into
Yugoslavian oakmoss absolute and orange flower
absolute from France to make *Madeleine de
Madeleine* one of the longest lasting perfumes in
the world.
Bottle Design: Gracefully packaged in a specially
designed diamond shaped glass bottle.
Pictured Size: .125oz.
Dimensions: 2" h x 3/4" w
CPG: $4.00

MARC DE LA MORANDIERE
Parfums Marc de la Morandiere, Paris

Other Madeleine Mono Fragrances

Mad Moments®
**"For the moments that are many and the
moments that are few"**
Launch Date: 1980s
Fragrance Type: Eau de Parfum: Floral, Rose,
Chypre.
Bottle Design: Gracefully packaged in a specially
designed diamond shaped glass bottle.
Package Design: The Victorian inspired box was
designed by Madeleine Mono from her personal
collection of Victorian memorabilia. This most
unusual *decoupaged* box with its clock faces,
hearts, cupids, and bows is in keeping with a
softer, gentler future that we are all searching for,
one of peace and tranquillity.

Sissi®
Launch Date: 1993
Fragrance Type: Eau de Toilette: Floral
Pictured Size: .30oz.
Dimensions: 2-1/8" h x 1-3/4" w
CPG: $15.00

MARILYN MIGLIN

Marilyn Miglin

DESTINY®
Launch Date: 1990
Fragrance Type: Perfume: Pure white flowers. This light, feminine fragrance blends the essential oils of seven pure white flowers.
Bottle Design: Faceted to express the upward movement of energy.
Pictured Size: .125oz.
Dimensions: 3" h x1" w
CPG: $12.50

M®
"Discover the most powerful attraction known to woman."
Launch Date: 1994
Fragrance Type: Aftershave/Cologne: Inspired by the male rituals of ancient Mesopotamia. This men's fragrance is a warm, rich scent made from rare essential oils that heighten sensual and intellectual response.
Pictured Size: .125oz.
Dimensions: 3" h x 3/4" w
CPG: $30.00 (Gift Set Purchase)

MAGIC®
"Mystery and possibilities."
Launch Date: 1995
Pictured Size: .125oz.
Dimensions: 2" h x 3/4" w
CPG: $30.00 (Gift Set Purchase)

Pheromone®
"The world's most precious perfume"
Launch Date: 1979
Fragrance Type: Perfume: Pheromone's vibrant blend of ingredients include florals, wild grasses, and rare wine resins. Heart notes are a variety of exotic florals blended with base notes of woody, mossy, and powdery notes.
Bottle Design: Egyptian obelisk.
Pictured Size: .125oz.
Dimensions: 2-1/2" h x 3/4" w
CPG: $15.00

MÄURER & WIRTZ
Lippens Inc. International

Tabac Original®
Launch Date: 1959
Fragrance Type: Eau de Toilette: Rich, ostentatious, tenacious, with a note of freshness which gives a feeling of well-being.
Pictured Size: .16oz.
Dimensions: 2" h x 1" w
CPG: $5.00

Other Mäurer & Wirtz Fragrances

Nonchalance®
Launch Date: 1960
Fragrance Type: Floral

Tabac Extreme®
Launch Date: 1990
Fragrance Type: Chypre-Citrus.

MAX FACTOR & CO.

Max Factor, Sr.

Epris™
Launch Date: 1981
Fragrance Type: Parfum: Citrus notes are blended with floral middle notes. Base notes are sweet and powdery.
Pictured Size: .12oz.
Dimensions: 1-3/4" h x 1" w
CPG: $4.00

Hypnotique™
Launch Date: 1958
Fragrance Type: Perfume
Pictured Size: .125oz.
Dimensions: 2" h x 3/4" w
CPG: $2.00

Le Jardin de Max Factor™
Launch Date: 1983
Fragrance Type: Eau de Toilette: Fruity top notes blended together with light floral middle notes. Base notes are powdery and woody.
Pictured Size: .12oz.
Dimensions: 2-1/8" h x 1-1/4" w
CPG: $4.00

Other Max Factor Fragrances

Aquarius™
Launch Date: 1970
Fragrance Type: Top notes are spicy and citrusy.
Middle notes are florals with base notes that are
leathery and woody.

Blasé™
Launch Date: 1975
Fragrance Type: Top notes are citrusy with
florals. Middle notes are florals with base notes
that are sensual and powdery.

Electrique™
Launch Date: November, 1954

Geminesse™
Launch Date: 1974
Fragrance Type: Top notes are citrusy and floral.
Middle notes of florals are blended with sweet,
mossy, and ambered base notes.

Le Jardin de d'Amour™
Launch Date: 1983
Fragrance Type: Floral-Aldehydic.

Magical Musk by Toujours Moi™
Launch Date: 1984

Miss Factor™
Launch Date: 1973
Fragrance Type: Citrus oils are blended with a
hint of floral as top notes. Sweet floral middle
notes are blended with balsamic, powdery, mossy
base notes.

Primitif™
Launch Date: November, 1956
Fragrance Type: Parfum

Toujours Moi™
Launch Date: 1921 (Reintroduced by Max Factor
in 1961)
Fragrance Type: Parfum
Bottle Design: Trial size sample bottle when Max
Factor bought rights from Corday.

MAXIM'S
Maxim's de Paris

Maxims de Paris®
Launch Date: 1985
Fragrance Type: Parfum: Fruity and floral notes
blend with notes that are ambered, mossy, and
musky.
Pictured Size: .14oz.
Dimensions: 1-3/4 " h x 1-1/2" w
CPG: $5.00

Mediterraneum

Mediterraneum®
Launch Date: 1993
Fragrance Type: EDT Pour Homme: Oriental-Spicy.
Pictured Size: .25oz.
Dimensions: 2-1/2" h x 1-1/4" w
CPG: $5.00

Merle Norman Cosmetics

Décolleté®
Launch Date: 1987 (U.S.A.)
Fragrance Type: Perfume: A very elegant designer fragrance, Décolleté is a floral, chypre scent. This modern creation, made with the finest natural essences, harmoniously captures the elegance and richness of a classical fragrance with the originality and strength of a modern perfume. The fresh top note (tangerine oil, bergamot oil) develops into a full-bodied floral note composed of the highest quality absolutes (jasmine, tuberose, and rose). This harmony of notes constitutes the main character of this fragrance. Aldehydes add a pleasant nuance to this bouquet. Woody notes (vetiver from Bourbon Island and patchouli from Singapore) compliment the floral body and suggest a vanilla (vanilla infusion) and animal drydown (civet absolute, castoreum resin) which is very long-lasting.
Pictured Size: .14oz.
Dimensions: 1-1/4" h x 1-1/2" w
CPG: $10.00

> **Fun Facts**
> on Décolleté®
> The French word Décolleté means to
> uncover the neck & shoulders.

MISSONI

Molto Missoni®
Launch Date: 1990
Fragrance Type: Eau de Toilette: Oriental-Ambered.
Pictured Size: .12oz.
Dimensions: 1-1/4" h x 1-1/4" w
CPG: $5.00

MOLINARD
Parfums Molinard

Habanita®
Launch Date: 1920
Fragrance Type: Parfum: Top notes are fruity while the heart of this fragrance is sweet and floral. Base notes are sweet, powdery, and balsamic.
Pictured Size: .25oz.
Dimensions: 2-1/4" h x 2" w
CPG: $9.00

Molinard de Molinard®
Launch Date: 1980 (Reintroduced)
Fragrance Type: Parfum: Top notes include galbanum, spearmint, marigold, bergamot, pineapple, and raspberry. Middle notes are floral notes of jasmine, lily of the valley, tuberose, cyclamen, melon, and orange blossom. Mossy base notes include musk, oakmoss, and cedarwood.
Pictured Size: .16oz.
Dimensions: 2-1/8" h x 1-1/4" w
CPG: $12.00

Namiko®
Launch Date: 1930s
Fragrance Type: "Perfume Wick"
Casing: These small perfume wicks were painted with floral images on cap (not shown here).
Pictured Size: Scented Wick
Dimensions: 3/4" h x1" w
CPG: $12.00

Other Molinard Fragrances

1811®
Launch Date: 1930
Fragrance Type: Created to celebrate the birth of Napoleon's son.

Calendal®
Launch Date: 1929
Fragrance Type: Warm, flowery fragrance.

Le Baiser du Faune®
Launch Date: 1930
Fragrance Type: Warm, flowery fragrance.

Les Iscles d'Or®
Launch Date: 1930
Fragrance Type: Warm, flowery fragrance.

Madrigal®
Launch Date: 1935
Fragrance Type: Floral fragrance.

Nirmala®
Launch Date: 1955
Fragrance Type: Warm, flowery fragrance.

Rafale®
Launch Date: 1975
Fragrance Type: Fresh, fruity top notes are blended with radiant light floral middle notes. Base notes are mossy and powdery.

Xmas Bells®
Launch Date: 1926
Fragrance Type: Warm, flowery fragrance.
Bottle Design: Black bell decorated with gold threading around neck of bottle and gold tone lettering.

MOLYNEUX
Edward Henri Molyneux
Molyneux Perfumes, Paris

Captain®
"An invitation to a voyage."
Launch Date: 1975
Fragrance Type: Eau de Toilette: Citrus-Woodsy. Top notes are pine, lemon, verbena, lavender, and rosemary. Heart notes of clove, nutmeg, coriander, tobacco, moss, patchouli, and sandalwood blended with base notes of civet and musk. A masculine fragrance named in honor of Edward Molyneux. A young and modern perfume for the active, dynamic man who strives for well-being and possesses refinement. *Captain* allies power and tenderness, unites force with gentleness.
Pictured Size: .25oz.
Dimensions: 2-3/4" h x 1-1/8" w
CPG: $9.00

Other Molyneux Fragrances

Charm®
Launch Date: 1929

Fête®
Launch Date: 1962
Fragrance Type: Fruity-Floral.

Gauloise®
Launch Date: 1981
Fragrance Type: Florals with an oriental note and woody, spicy base notes.

Le Chic®
Launch Date: 1932

Magnificence®
Launch Date: 1936

Rue Royale®
Launch Date: 1938

Vivre®
Launch Date: 1971
Fragrance Type: Florals with sandalwood, vetiver, and oak moss.

Vogue®
Launch Date: 1930

Quartz®
Launch Date: 1978
Fragrance Type: Eau de Parfum: The fragrance Quartz belongs to the floral-fruity family. From the outset, its freshness is enveloping and becomes irresistible when floral notes are mixed with it. Top notes of lemon, tangerine, bergamot, and pineapple rind blend with heart notes of iris, jasmine, lily of the valley, honeysuckle, and rose. Base notes are graminaceous, sandalwood, patchouli, and Tyrolese moss. This exquisite Eau de Parfum is meant to appeal to the untamed, haughty, and elusive woman. The Quartz woman is free, dazzling, contemporary.
Bottle Design: The perfume bottle is different: modern, with pure lines, distinguished by its understatedness.
Pictured Size: .25oz.
Dimensions: 2" h x 1-1/8" w
CPG: $7.00

MONTANA
Claude Montana
Montana Parfums
Lippens Inc. International

Montana™ Parfum De Peau
Launch Date: 1986
Fragrance Type: Parfum de Peau: Top notes—cold colors—blues, greens with a sharp, spicy, fresh,

...d dry departure. A mixture of ginger, pepper, ...ssis, and orange. The heart is a bouquet of floral ...otes of jasmine, rose, and narcissus bloom ...mong woody notes of patchouli, sandalwood, and ...akmoss. The base notes remind one of warmer ...ades brown, copper, and gold. A regal blend— ...ather moving towards musk to ash and amber. ...ich fabrics, suedes, cashmeres, silks, and linens ...re suggested by the note of leather.

Bottle Design: Spiral of life dressed in Klein Blue.
Pictured Size: .07oz.
Dimensions: 1" h x 1-1/4" w
CPG: $10.00

Montana™ *Parfum D'Homme*

Launch Date: 1986
Fragrance Type: Eau de Toilette: Fresh-Spicy-Woody. Top notes— hesperides theme of tangerine, bergamot orange, and lemon with a spicy theme of cinnamon, pepper, and nutmeg. Heart notes begin with a floral theme of jasmine, geranium, and nasturtium with an agrestic theme of sage and a woody theme of patchouli and sandalwood. Base notes with a balsamic theme of ambergris, incense, and citrus and a musky theme of civet and musk.

Bottle Design: Sculptured flacon, Tower of Babel of the Future, the *Parfum D'Homme* bottles with their contour of matte-golden bronze set in Etruscan red are a visual shock. Marked with the double imprint of the Sculptor and the Architect, they transcribe the power of the ascendant Spiral of Enthusiasm, the upwards path to the ideal. Matte-golden bronze, the color of legends, evokes Eternity, Dignity, and Determination.

Package Design: The cases bear the mark of Enthusiasm, Energy, and Conquest. This is the strength of Etruscan red.
Pictured Size: .13oz.
Dimensions: Sample Vial Pictured

MONTEIL
Germaine Monteil
Monteil Paris

Bakir®

Launch Date: 1975
Fragrance Type: Perfume: Spicy and fruity accords create the top notes while middle notes are spicy and floral. Base notes are sensual orientals.
Pictured Size: .5oz.
Dimensions: 2-1/2" h x 1-1/2" w
CPG: $4.00

Germaine®
Launch Date: 1971
Fragrance Type: Perfume: Fresh, flowery top notes and green accords blend with elegant floral middle notes and base notes that are sensual and feminine.
Pictured Size: .25oz.
Dimensions: 2-1/4" h x 1-1/8" w
CPG: $6.00

Royal Secret®
Launch Date: 1958
Fragrance Type: Eau de Parfum: Fresh, citrusy top notes with a hint of spice blended into exotic floral middle notes that end with sweet, ambery, and powdery base notes.
Pictured Size: .25oz.
Dimensions: 3" h x 3/4" w
CPG: $8.00

Fun Facts
on Germaine Monteil
She was a very famous and celebrated French fashion designer.

Other Monteil Fragrances

Champagne®
Launch Date: 1983

Galore®
Launch Date: Undetermined

L'Eau de Monteil®
Launch Date: Fall, 1995
Fragrance Type: Eau de Parfum: Floral

MORABITO
Pascal Morabito
Parfums Morabito

Mon Classique®
Launch Date: 1987
Fragrance Type: Perfume: Floral
Pictured Size: .14oz.
Dimensions: 2-1/8" h x1-1/2" w
CPG: $6.00

Other Morabito Fragrances

Or Noir®
Launch Date: 1981
Fragrance Type: Fresh herbaceous notes establish the top notes. Precious and exotic floral middle notes blend with sensual, feminine, woody base notes.

Turquoise®
Launch Date: Undetermined

MOSCHINO
Franco Moschino
H. Alpert & Company, Inc.

Moschino® Pour Homme
Launch Date: 1990
Fragrance Type: Eau de Toilette: Chypre-Leathery: notes of coriander, gardenia, rose, carnation, and spices with woody notes, vanilla, amber, and musk.
Bottle Design: Scotch bottle design.
Pictured Size: .125oz.
Dimensions: 2-1/4" h x 3/4" w
CPG: $8.00

Other Moschino Fragrances

Parfum Moschino®
Launch Date: 1987
Fragrance Type: Oriental-Ambered.

MYRURGIA
Myrurgia Parfums

Maja®
Launch Date: 1918
Fragrance Type: Eau de Toilette: Literally, the word Maja is derived from May, the month of the flowers. Figuratively, the word Maja is also used to express the maximum extremes of feminine beauty. "Maja" is art. The fragrance was created to spark your inner being. A legendary perfume that is the heart and soul of Spain. Passionate. Exciting. Sensual. Top notes are Bulgarian rose, Egyptian geranium, carnation, and tuberose. Middle notes are Madagascar clove, ceylon, nutmeg, and French cassis. Base notes are patchouli, amber, and vetiver.
Package Design: The representative figure of the Spanish woman is pictured on the package. Many artists have represented her, but Francisco Jose de Goya, one of the most brilliant Spanish artists, immortalized her in his painting "Maja Desnuda".
Pictured Size: .25oz.
Dimensions: 2-3/4" h x 1-1/8" w
CPG: $8.00

Other Myrurgia Fragrances

Embrujo de Sevilla®
Launch Date: 1933
Fragrance Type: Floral-Aldehydic: Fruity, citrusy accents define the top notes while elegant florals create the middle notes. Base notes are sensual, woody, and powdery.

Flor de Blason®
Launch Date: 1926
Fragrance Type: Top notes are herbaceous with floral middle notes. Base notes are sweet and powdery with a hint of spice.

Joya®
Launch Date: 1950
Fragrance Type: Floral-Aldehydic: Fresh, citrusy top notes, classic floral middle notes and warm, balsamic base notes.

Maderas de Oriente®
Launch Date: 1920
Fragrance Type: Fresh, spicy top notes blend into luscious spicy, floral middle notes. Base notes are floral and powdery.

Nueva Maja®
Launch Date: 1960
Fragrance Type: Chypre: Top notes are fresh and citrusy. Spicy, florals accent the heart notes while base notes are balsamic.

Orgia®
Launch Date: 1922
Fragrance Type: Aldehydic accords compliment the soft, feminine floral heart. Base notes are powdery and woody.

Perfume Alado®
Launch Date: 1926
Fragrance Type: Citrusy top notes and heart notes of fresh florals blend into base notes that are woody and mossy.

Fun Facts
Worth More Than Money
During the 11th century, cloves were in such demand for everything from cooking to medicine that they were used in bartering in place of coined currency.

NICOLE MILLER
Riviera Concepts Inc.

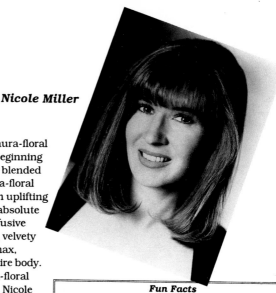

Nicole Miller

Nicole Miller®
Launch Date: October, 1993
Fragrance Type: Parfum: An explosive, aura-floral fragrance. A sparkling fragrance design beginning with bright effusive top notes of carefully blended mandarin, freesia, and cyclamen. An aura-floral bouquet of radiant heart notes provide an uplifting weave of rich florals including tuberose, absolute rose, jasmine, and lilac. The serenely diffusive bottom notes blend the exquisite creamy, velvety notes of sandalwood, vanilla, and opopanax, draping a fragrant silhouette over the entire body.
Bottle Design: To Nicole Miller, her aura-floral fragrance is a jewel. To capture this gem, Nicole Miller and Pierre Dinand created a treasured pouch. A true reflection of Nicole's sense of fun, the fragrance bottle is soft and sophisticated. The gentle curves, gold cord, and stopper cap encase the sexy, feminine fragrance.
Package Design: Surrounding the bottle is an elegant matte black box. The gold tassel and trompe-l'ceil lines mirror the bottle—a "pouch of perfume."
Pictured Size: .17oz. (Deluxe Miniature Size)
Dimensions: 2-1/4" h x 1" w
CPG: $12.50

> ***Fun Facts***
> on Nicole Miller®
> "Nicole Miller's experiment of making 36 ties from an unsuccessful dress print launched her career in the whimsical world of men's fashion."
> Riviera Concepts, Inc.

Nicole Miller® for Men

Launch Date: October, 1994

Fragrance Type: Eau de Toilette: *Nicole Miller for Men* is a modern, fresh, warm oriental fragrance, inspired by a textural twist. Her fashion is stimulated by design and translated into fabric and fragrance. Inspired by the rugged textural smell of "GUY THINGS" like a BASEBALL MITT and LEATHER LOAFERS, this fragrance captures the smooth softness of NUBUCK LEATHER. Crisp top notes of bergamot, lemon, honeydew, and apple provide the perfect introduction to the rich and leathery mid note accord of bourbon, jasmine, okoumal, and leather. Smooth and sensual base notes of sandalwood, vanilla, opopanax, tobacco, and oak moss, add to the "GUY THINGS" accord by enhancing its warm textural quality and increasing its endurance.

Bottle Design: To complement Nicole Miller's treasured "perfume pouch," Nicole Miller for Men is whimsically reflected in a rugged bottle and box. The frosted amber bottle appears unidentified like her "pouch of perfume," however both bottles are unmistakably Nicole Miller.

Package Design: Contemporary corrugated contours encase the fresh essence of *Nicole Miller for Men* inside and out.

Available Size: .24 fl. oz. (Deluxe Miniature Size)

Dimensions: 2-3/8" h x 1" w

CPG: $12.00

Niki de Saint Phalle

Niki de Saint Phalle®

Launch Date: 1983

Fragrance Type: Perfume: Chypre-Floral.

Bottle Design: The multi-colored serpent on the perfume bottle (the female) is hand painted; the gold serpent is the male. The Eau de Toilette flacons are silk-screened in six colors with the signature serpent logo.

Pictured Size: .17oz.

Dimensions: 2" h x 1-1/2" w

CPG: $7.00

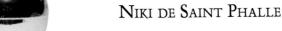

Fun Facts
on Niki de Saint Phalle
"Niki de Saint Phalle, one of the *foremost women artists* of our time, has been called a genius and a witch, probably the truth lies somewhere in between."
Fragrance Marketing Group

NINA RICCI
Nina Ricci Parfums

"Coeur-joie"®
Launch Date: 1946
Fragrance Type: Eau de Toilette: Floral
Pictured Size: .33oz.
Dimensions: 2-3/8" h x 1-3/4" w
CPG: $8.00

Farouche®
(Fierce and Shy)
Launch Date: 1974
Fragrance Type: Eau de Toilette: Top notes are
leafy green and fruity notes. Light florals create the
heart notes and soft, feminine, powdery notes
create the base notes.
Pictured Size: .25oz.
Dimensions: 2-1/4" h x 1-1/2" w
CPG: $8.00

L'Air du Temps®
Launch Date: 1948
Fragrance Type: Parfum: Top notes are fresh,
flowery, and spicy with spicy, floral notes at the
heart. The base notes are mild, powdery notes that
are very feminine.
Bottle Design: Single dove stopper design dates
before double dove stopper.
Pictured Size: .10 fl oz.
Dimensions: 1-3/4" h x 3/4" w
CPG: $10.00

L'Air du Temps®
Launch Date: 1948
Pictured Size: .11 fl oz.
Dimensions: 1-3/4" h x 3/4" w
CPG: $7.00

L'Air du Temps®
Launch Date: 1948
Pictured Size: .25oz.
Dimensions: 2-1/8" h x 1-1/2" w
CPG: $75.00 - $95.00 (with casing)

Nina®
Launch Date: 1987
Fragrance Type: Eau de Toilette: Floral
Pictured Size: .25oz.
Dimensions: 1-3/8" h x 1-3/4" w
CPG: $12.00

Ricci Club®
Launch Date: 1989
Fragrance Type: Eau de Toilette: Oriental-Spicy.
Pictured Size: .5oz.
Dimensions: 2-1/8" h x 1" w
CPG: $6.00

Signoricci 1®
Launch Date: 1965
Fragrance Type: Eau de Toilette: Chypre-Fresh.
Pictured Size: .25oz.
Dimensions: 2" h x 1" w
CPG: $6.00

Other Nina Ricci Fragrances

Capricci®
Launch Date: 1961
Fragrance Type: Top notes are fresh florals and green leaves. The heart of this fragrance is a blend of exotic florals with the base notes of soft, powdery notes.

Eau de Fleurs®
Launch Date: 1980

Deci Delà®
Launch Date: 1995
Fragrance Type: Fruity, floral, and chypre notes.

Fleur de Fleurs®
Launch Date: 1982
Fragrance Type: Floral: Top notes have a hint of citrus notes and leafy greens. Delicate florals are at the heart with soft, powdery, florals at the base.

La Fille d'Eve®
Launch Date: 1952
Bottle Design: Frosted Apple.

Mademoiselle Ricci®
Launch Date: 1967
Fragrance Type: Fresh green notes of exotic floral middle notes. Mild, floral, and powdery notes create the base notes.

Phileas®
Launch Date: 1984
Fragrance Type: Cypress oak moss, mandarin, and lemon.

Signoricci 2 ®
Launch Date: 1976
Fragrance Type: Chypre

Nino Cerruti

Nino Cerruti®
Launch Date: 1979
Fragrance Type: Eau de Toilette: Sweet, floral notes with a warm, sensual background of patchouli, incense, and sandalwood.
Pictured Size: .25oz.
Dimensions: 2-3/4" h x 1-1/2" w
CPG: $8.00

Other Nino Cerruti Fragrances

Fair Play®
Launch Date: 1984
Fragrance Type: Peppermint, lavender, and bergamot with the woody essences of oak moss and musk.

Nino Cerruti 1881® for Men
Launch Date: 1990
Fragrance Type: Classical scent of ylang-ylang, sandalwood, and musk notes.

No. 4711
Richard Barrie Fragrances, Inc.

4711 Eau de Cologne®
Launch Date: 1792
Fragrance Type: Eau de Cologne: Sandalwood oil from India gives the fragrance its subtle exotic touch, attar of roses from Bulgaria contributes the light floral notes, and vetiver oil from Haiti adds a delicate spring-grass freshness. Bergamot, lemon, and orange oils gives 4711 its classic citrus notes and remarkably refreshing scent.
Pictured Size: .27oz.
*Can also be found in .10oz.
Dimensions: 2-1/8" h x 1" w
CPG: $4.00

Other 4711 Fragrances

**Please note that <u>none</u> of the below listed fragrances are distributed by Richard Barrie Fragrances, Inc.

Amun®
Launch Date: 1981
Fragrance Type: Spicy oils and fruity top notes are blended together with spicy, exotic floral middle notes. Base notes are sweet, ambered, and balsamic.

Jacuranda®
Launch Date: 1971
Fragrance Type: Fresh spicy, fruity top notes are blended together with precious floral middle notes. Base notes are warm, mossy, and woody.

Janine D.®
Launch Date: 1976
Fragrance Type: Fresh green top notes are blended together with light floral middle notes. Base notes are ambered and powdery.

Première®
Launch Date: 1981
Fragrance Type: Fruity, citrusy top notes lead the way to the elegant floral heart with warm powdery base notes.

My Melody®
Launch Date: 1979
Fragrance Type: Fresh, fruity notes with green accords create the top notes. Radiant florals are blended with ambered, powdery base notes.

Tosca®
Launch Date: 1921
Fragrance Type: Hints of citrus and floral top notes blend into heart notes of classic florals and base notes that are sweet and powdery.

OSCAR DE LE RENTA

Oscar de la Renta®
Launch Date: 1977
Fragrance Type: Parfum: Top notes are floral blend with sweet floral heart notes and base notes that are powdery and sensual.
Bottle Design: Frosted flower-like stopper with a crystal dewdrop. Represents the essence it contains.
Pictured Size: .14oz.
Dimensions: 1-3/4" h x 1-1/8" w
CPG: $8.00

Pour Lui®
Launch Date: 1980
Fragrance Type: Eau de Toilette: floral and mossy top notes blend with woody, spicy, and herbaceous notes.
Pictured Size: .33oz.
Dimensions: 3" h x 1" w
CPG: $4.00

Ruffles®
Launch Date: 1983
Fragrance Type: Eau de Parfum: Fruity and floral top notes are blended with exotic floral heart notes. Spicy, woody notes create the base notes.
Pictured Size: .14oz.
Dimensions: 1-3/4" h x 1-3/4" w
CPG: $10.00

Ruffles®
Launch Date: 1983
Fragrance Type: Eau de Toilette
Pictured Size: .17oz.
Dimensions: 1-1/2" h x 1-1/4" w
CPG: $8.00

Volupté®
Launch Date: April, 1992
Fragrance Type: Parfum: Floral
Pictured Size: .12oz.
Dimensions: 1-1/4" h x 1-1/2" w
CPG: $15.00

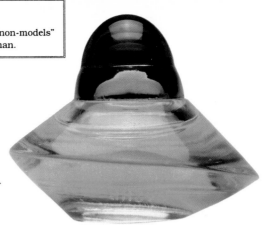

OTTO KERN

Noa Noa®
Launch Date: 1990
Fragrance Type: Eau de Toilette: Oriental-
Ambered.
Pictured Size: .17oz.
Dimensions: 2-1/4" h x 1-1/8" w
CPG: $6.00

PACO RABANNE
Paco Rabanne Parfums, Inc.

La Nuit®
Launch Date: 1985
Fragrance Type: Eau de Parfum: Fruity-Floral.
Pictured Size: .17oz.
Dimensions: 3" h x 1" w
CPG: $8.00

Paco Rabanne® Pour Homme
Launch Date: 1973
Fragrance Type: Eau de Toilette: Fougère: Woody and ambered.
Pictured Size: .17oz.
Dimensions: 2" h x 1-1/8" w
CPG: $5.00

Ténéré®
Launch Date: 1988
Fragrance Type: Eau de Toilette: Fougère: Woody and ambered.
Pictured Size: .17oz.
Dimensions: 2" h x 1-1/4" w
CPG: $6.00

Other Paco Rabanne Fragrances

Calandre®
Launch Date: 1969
Fragrance Type: Cool green leaves and flowery notes create the top notes while radiant floral middle notes lead the way to woody, mossy base notes.

Metal®
Launch Date: 1979
Fragrance Type: Fresh top notes are citrus oils and green accords. Base notes are soft florals and powdery notes.

XS®
Launch Date: 1993
Fragrance Type: Warm, spicy, and ambered.

XS Pour Elle®
Launch Date: 1995
Fragrance Type: Floral

Fun Facts
on XS Pour Elle®
Surfing the Internet for Cyberscents? Just punch in the right keys on your computer and place your order for *XS Pour Elle*.

PACOMA
Pacoma Perfumer

Swann®
Launch Date: 1984
Fragrance Type: Eau de Toilette: Floral
Pictured Size: .125oz.
Dimensions: 2-1/8" h x 1-1/4" w
CPG: $5.00

PALOMA PICASSO
Parfums Paloma Picasso

Minotaure®
Launch Date: 1992
Fragrance Type: Eau de Toilette: Fougère: Woody and ambered.
Pictured Size: .17oz.
Dimensions: 1-3/4" h x 1-1/8" w
CPG: $7.00

Paloma Picasso®
Launch Date: 1984
Fragrance Type: Eau de Parfum: Intoxicating florals and exotic woods create this rare fragrance.
Bottle Design: A crystal sphere enclosed in a black casing. Inspired by a pair of black palm wood earrings said to be a favored pair by Paloma.
Pictured Size: .25oz.
Dimensions: 1-3/4" h x 1-3/4" w
CPG: $10.00

PARADISO

L'Homme de Paradisio®
Launch Date: Undetermined
Fragrance Type: Eau de Toilette
Pictured Size: .25oz.
Dimensions: 2-1/2" h x 1" w
CPG: $6.00

PARFUMS CAFE
Parfums Cafe - Paris

Flor de Cafe®
Launch Date: Undetermined
Fragrance Type: Eau de Toilette
Pictured Size: .10oz.
Dimensions: 2" h x 1" w
CPG: $4.00

PARFUMS CREATIFS
distributed by Avon Products, Inc.

Casbah®
Launch Date: August, 1993
Fragrance Type: Eau de Toilette Deluxe Petite: Created by top perfumer Jean-Pierre Subrenat to express women's most romantic moods, *Casbah* is an oriental of opulent citrus, floral, spice, and wood notes.
Bottle Design: Deep blue glass is rendered by master designer Pierre Dinand into a flacon that echoes the mystery of the fragrance within. Collared in a wide golden band and capped with a frosted blue oval.
Package Design: *Casbah* is boxed in stylish blue-on-blue, crisscrossed in gold.
Pictured Size: .13oz.
Dimensions: 1-1/2" h x 1-3/4" w
CPG: $8.00

C'est moi!®

Launch Date: August, 1993

Fragrance Type: Eau de Toilette Deluxe Petite: Created by world class perfumer Jean-Pierre Subrenat. Memorable and effervescent as an April morning in Paris, *C'est moi!*, bursting with a brilliant white floral bouquet and fruity, citrus, precious wood, and herbal notes is a spirited, full-of-life fragrance for vivacious, confident women.

Bottle Design: An up sweep of clear and frosted glass is topped with a golden knob and capped in translucent chartreuse. The crystalline flacon allows *C'est moi!* to show its heart of pale, rain-washed green—by award winning designer, Pierre Dinand.

Package Design: The flacon is presented in a spring green and white box banded with gold.

Pictured Size: .13oz.

Dimensions: 2" h x 1-1/2" w

CPG: $8.00

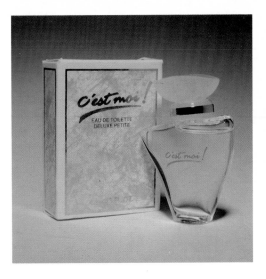

Perle noire®

Launch Date: August, 1993

Fragrance Type: Eau de Toilette Deluxe Petite: Created by Jean-Pierre Subrenat. A rich, warm floriental, it enticingly combines rare floral and fruit essences with seductive, lingering woody notes.

Bottle Design: A half-moon crystal-clear bottle, gleaming with *Perle noire's* amber light, is crowned with a slender band and sinuously carved black cap. Designed by Pierre Dinand.

Package Design: The flacon is elegantly presented in a black-on-black box.

Pictured Size: .13oz.

Dimensions: 1-1/2" h x 1-3/4" w

CPG: $8.00

Pierre Dinand

Jean-Pierre Subrenat

PAUL SEBASTIAN

Design®
Launch Date: Undetermined
Fragrance Type: Parfum
Pictured Size: .25oz.
Dimensions: 2-3/4" h x 3/4" w
CPG: $26.00 (Gift set)

PAYOT

Pavlova®
Launch Date: 1976
Fragrance Type: Parfum: Top notes of fruity and green accords accent the heart notes of exotic florals and fruits blended with soft, powdery, woody base notes.
Pictured Size: .06oz.
Dimensions: 1-1/2" h x 3/4" w
CPG: $4.00

> **Fun Facts**
> A Prima Fragrance
> Inspired by the famous ballerina Pavlova.

PERFUMES OF HAWAII
by Langer

bleu Hawaii®
Launch Date: June, 1983
Fragrance Type: Perfume: bleu Hawaii is the uniquely different essence creation from the Hawaiian Islands. The fragrance, decidedly Polynesian, blends the freshness of citrus top notes along with full bodied mossy and woody notes to create an unforgettable Island experience.
Pictured Size: .5oz.
Dimensions: 3-3/4" h x 1" w
CPG: $21.00

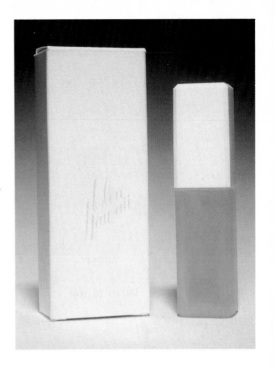

Other Perfumes of Hawaii Fragrances

Hawaiian Blue®
Launch Date: April, 1984
Fragrance Type: A fresh fragrance in the classic tradition of men's scents. Subtly masculine and provocatively appealing with just a hint of lime, it was created by Perfumes of Hawaii for a lifestyle that embraces the outdoors and celebrates nature.

Hawaiian Carnation®
Launch Date: June, 1983
Fragrance Type: The "happy flower" of Hawaii, Carnations are grown on the lush mountain slopes of Kula of the Island of Maui. Called ponimo'i in Hawaiian, carnations are prized for their gentle scent. The blossoms are most often used to make white, red, or pink leis given out on special happy occasions.

Hawaiian Jasmine®
Launch Date: October, 1978
Fragrance Type: The tiny Hawaiian Jasmine blossom is called Pikake in the Islands. For centuries Pikake leis have been worn by Hawaiian brides for the unforgettable fragrance and the ivory beauty of the blossom. The Pikake is the fragrance of romance.

Hawaiian Gardenia®
Launch Date: October, 1978
Fragrance Type: The Gardenia of the Hawaiian Isles is a rare beauty in both form and fragrance, growing to perfection in this balmy climate. The warm days and cool nights combine to make this unique Gardenia very white and very fragrant. It is the exotic blossom of Hawaii.

Hawaiian Orchid®
Launch Date: October, 1978
Fragrance Type: The Hawaiian Orchid is probably the most often thought of blossom of Hawaii. The lovely lavender and light yellow colors have for years made it the royal flower of our Islands. This delightful fragrance is as beautiful as the flower itself.

Hawaiian Hibiscus®
Launch Date: October, 1978
Fragrance Type: The Hibiscus is found throughout the Hawaiian Islands, often behind some pretty Hawaiian girl's ear. As custom has it, if it's behind the left ear she's taken; behind the right one, she's looking! This proud flower with its variety of colors is the pride of Hawaii and is the official State flower.

Hawaiian Plumeria®
Launch Date: October, 1978
Fragrance Type: The most popular Hawaiian leis are made of this velvety flower. Whether in a lei or a single blossom, the clear yellow and creamy white petals yield a lovely fragrance. The Plumeria is known as the Melia by Polynesians and blooms the year 'round.

Hawaiian White Ginger®
Launch Date: October, 1978
Fragrance Type: The White Ginger with its moon-white blossoms has a never to be forgotten delicate fragrance. The White Ginger grows wild in the high rain forests of Hawaii and carries with it the warm scent of tropical stillness.

Maile® for Men
Launch Date: April, 1984
Fragrance Type: A unique scent from the Hawaiian Islands, created for the adventurous man. So subtle, so unconventional...Maile (pronounced MY-lee) grows deep in the tropical forest of Hawaii and in ancient days, the vines were gathered and twisted into leis reserved for royalty. Even today, Maile leis are reserved for the most special occasions, and to be presented with a Maile lei is to be shown singular honor and respect.

Hawaiian Rose®
Launch Date: October, 1978
Fragrance Type: From the Valley Isle of Maui comes the fragrant Lokelani or Hawaiian Rose. Its brilliant color and delicate fragrance have long made it a favorite of Polynesia. You will love this unique scent as you will delight in the scarlet blossom.

Hawaiian Tiare®
Launch Date: June, 1983
Fragrance Type: The exotic Tiare flower is a favorite in Hawaii and throughout all of Polynesia. The pure white petals and its distinctive scent make the Tiare blossom a favorite of Island ladies who wear them for social and festive occasions.

Hawaiian Tuberose®
Launch Date: June, 1983
Fragrance Type: In Hawaii, the Tuberose blossom is often used in making flower leis. The warm scent of this delicate flower will bring back beautiful memories of the Islands.

PERFUMER'S WORKSHOP

Rosebud®
Launch Date: Spring, 1994
Fragrance Type: Parfum: Floral
Pictured Size: .17oz.
Dimensions: 2-1/2" h x 1-1/4" w
CPG: $7.00

Parfum Tea Rose®
Launch Date: 1970
Fragrance Type: Parfum: Floral
Pictured Size: .17oz.
Dimensions: 2-1/2" h x 1-1/4" w
CPG: $5.00

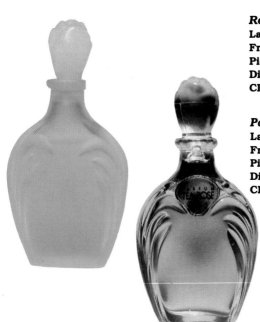

Samba Parfum® for Women

From Left to Right:
Samba Parfum Espirit de Parfum®,
Samba Nova Espirit de Parfum®,
Samba Nova Eau de Toilette®,
Samba Eau de Toilette®
Launch Date: 1992
Bottle Design: Signature design of ring-upon-ring or doughnut ring.
Pictured Size: .25oz.
Dimensions: 1-1/8" h x 1-1/8" w
CPG: $5.00 (Individual bottles)

Samba Men's Collection®

From Left to Right:
Samba Nova Homme-EDT®,
Samba For Men-After Shave®,
Samba Nova Homme Sports Cologne®,
Samba For Men-EDT®,
Samba Nova Homme-After Shave®
Launch Date: 1992
Bottle Design: Signature design of ring-upon-ring or doughnut ring.
Pictured Size: .25oz.
Dimensions: 1-1/8" h x 1-1/8" w
CPG: $5.00 (Individual bottles)

PERRY ELLIS
Parlux Fragrances, Inc.

360º®
"Life is how you change it"
Launch Date: 1993
Fragrance Type: Fresh, floral musk.
Bottle Design: Round sphere mirroring the parfum bottle presentation.
Package Design: Cool white with gold border.
Pictured Size: .12oz.
Dimensions: 1-1/8" h x 1-1/8" w
CPG: $9.00

Perry Ellis® for Women
Launch Date: 1986
Fragrance Type: Eau de Toilette: Floral: Natural and sophisticated.
Bottle Design: Dramatic rounded rectangle with gold cap.
Package Design: Tiffany blue and white with Perry Ellis logo.
Pictured Size: .14oz.
Dimensions: 1-1/8" h x 1-3/4" w
CPG: $10.00

Perry Ellis® for Men
Launch Date: 1986
Fragrance Type: Eau de Toilette: Woody-Chypre.
Bottle Design: Dramatic rounded rectangle with black cap.
Package Design: Rust brown and black with Perry Ellis logo.
Pictured Size: .14oz.
Dimensions: 1-1/8" h x 1-3/4" w
CPG: $8.00

Other Perry Ellis Fragrances

360º® for Men
Launch Date: 1995
Fragrance Type: Fresh-Fougère.
Package Design: Gun metal gray with white accents.

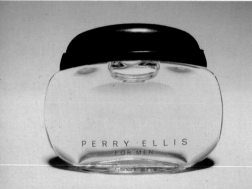

PIERRE BALMAIN
Pierre Balmain, Paris

Ivoire®
Launch Date: 1979
Fragrance Type: Eau de Toilette: Green notes are blended with floral middle notes and sensual, powdery base notes.
Pictured Size: .25oz.
Dimensions: 2" h x 1-3/4" w
CPG: $7.00

Jolie Madame®
Launch Date: 1953
Fragrance Type: Eau de Toilette: Spicy, floral top notes are blended with precious floral middle notes and warm, mossy, powdery, leathery base notes.
Pictured Size: .06oz.
Dimensions: 1-3/8" h x 3/4" w
CPG: $5.00

Vent Vert®
Launch Date: 1944 (Reintroduced 1992)
Fragrance Type: Eau de Toilette: Citrus oils, florals, and mossy notes create this fragrance.
Pictured Size: .13oz.
Dimensions: 2-3/8" h x 3/4" w
CPG: $7.00

```
Fun Facts
Vent Vert®
Means "Green Breeze"
```

211

Other Pierre Balmain Fragrances

Ebene®
Launch Date: 1967
Fragrance Type: Rich and musky fragrance for men, sage, cedar, sandal, and oak moss.

Miss Balmain®
Launch Date: 1967
Fragrance Type: Citrusy and herbaceous top notes are blended with precious floral middle notes and warm, ambered, leathery base notes.

Monsieur Balmain®
Launch Date: 1990
Fragrance Type: Fresh, brisk of citronella, orange, bergamot, lemon, and verbena.

PIERRE CARDIN
Parfums Pierre Cardin

Rose Cardin®
Launch Date: 1990
Fragrance Type: Eau de Parfum: Chypre
Pictured Size: .25oz.
Dimensions: 3-1/2" h x 1" w
CPG: $12.00

Other Pierre Cardin Fragrances

CARDIN de Pierre Cardin®
Launch Date: 1976
Fragrance Type: Floral-Fruity.

CHOC®
Launch Date: 1981
Fragrance Type: Citrusy, spicy, floral, woody, and mossy notes.

ENIGME®
Launch Date: 1992
Fragrance Type: Chypre-Leathery.

Insatiable®
Launch Date: Summer, 1995

Paradoxe®
Launch Date: 1983
Fragrance Type: Floral bouquet blended with leathery, mossy base notes.
Bottle Design: Circular bottle with bottom half of sphere a clear glass while top 1/2 sphere is solid stopper.

Pierre Cardin® Pour Homme
Launch Date: 1976
Fragrance Type: Eau de Toilette: Citrusy, spicy with warm amber notes.
Bottle Design: Cylinder bottle with sphere cap.

Fun Facts
on Pierre Cardin
Famous for his design of the bubble dress.

PIERRE LORAIN

dieci®
Launch Date: 1975
Fragrance Type: Perfume
Pictured Size: .125oz.
Dimensions: 2" h x 3/4" w
CPG: $4.00

PLAYBOY, INC.

Playmate®
Launch Date: c1960
Fragrance Type: Perfume
Pictured Size: .14oz.
Dimensions: 2-3/8" h x 3/4" w
CPG: $15.00

Fun Facts
on Playmate®
This was a perfume which was probably sold in the
Playboy Clubs as a novelty item,
along with pens, key chains, and cigarette lighters. All
clubs in the USA
are now closed. A history of these novelty items was
never kept.
Playboy Enterprises, Inc.

PRINCE DOUKA
Marquay, Paris

Prince Douka®
Launch Date: 1951
Fragrance Type: Perfume
Pictured Size: .25oz.
Dimensions: 2-1/8" h x 1" w
CPG: $15.00

Fun Facts
Fragrant Poetry
Still fragrant with the original rose perfumed pages,
the poems of Jami can be found in the Oxford Library.

PRINCE MATCHABELLI
Prince Georges Matchabelli

Abano®
Launch Date: 1938
Fragrance Type: Perfume Oil
Pictured Size: .20oz.
Dimensions: 2-1/2" h x 1" w
CPG: $4.00

From Left to Right:
Added Attraction®
1956
Golden Autumn®
1948
Prophecy®
c1950
Stradivari®
c1950
Wind Song®
1953
Pictured Size: .06oz.
Dimensions: 1-1/4" h x 1-1/8" w
CPG: $4.00 (Individual bottles—each of the above mentioned fragrances can be found in pictured crown bottles.)

> **Fun Facts**
> From Exiled to Exalted
> An exiled Russian Prince who made perfume for his friends as a hobby;
> his family's crown becoming the shape of the bottles.

Aviance®
Launch Date: 1975
Fragrance Type: Perfume: Leafy green notes lead the way to the heart of floral notes. Base notes are floral, woody, and powdery notes.
Pictured Size: .25oz.
Dimensions: 2-1/4" h x 1-1/8" w
CPG: $4.00

214

Aviance Night Musk®

Launch Date: 1970s
Fragrance Type: Perfume: Musk
Pictured Size: .25oz.
Dimensions: 2-1/4" h x 1-1/8" w
CPG: $5.00

Béret®

Launch Date: Undetermined
Fragrance Type: Cologne
Pictured Size: .25oz.
Dimensions: 2-3/8" h x 1-3/8" w
CPG: $3.00

Cachet®

Launch Date: 1970
Fragrance Type: Perfume: Luscious herbaceous
and spicy notes create the top notes. Middle notes
are floral with woody notes and base notes are
leathery, mossy, and ambered.
Pictured Size: .25oz.
Dimensions: 2" h x 1-1/8" w
CPG: $18.00

215

Chimère®
Launch Date: 1980
Fragrance Type: Perfume: Florals and green notes create the top notes. A floral heart of narcissus, rose, carnation, ylang-ylang, and jasmine with base notes that are woody and mossy.
Pictured Size: .07oz.
Dimensions: 2-3/8" h x 2" w
CPG: $6.00

Other Prince Matchabelli Fragrances

Luna Mystique®
Launch Date: 1990
Fragrance Type: Eau de Parfum
Pictured Size: .25oz.
Dimensions: 2-3/8" h x 2-1/4" w
CPG: $5.00

PRINCESSE DE MARINA DE BOURBON

Parfums Princesse Marina De Bourbon Parme

Princesse Marina De Bourbon®
Launch Date: Undetermined
Fragrance Type: Eau de Parfum
Pictured Size: .25oz.
Dimensions: 2-3/8" h x 2-1/2" w
CPG: $9.00

PRISCILLA PRESLEY
Richard Barrie Fragrances, Inc.

Experiences®
Launch Date: August, 1993
Fragrance Type: Eau de Toilette: The name of this fragrance is inspired as a "natural extension" of Priscilla Presley's multifaceted life. Selected roses, blended with lily of the valley and other florals, are strengthened by cedar at the fragrance's heart. Exotic sandalwood tinged with sensuous musk and rich amber add depth in the lasting bottom note.
Package Design: Cobalt blue packaging.
Pictured Size: .10oz.
Dimensions: 1-3/4" h x 1-1/2" w
CPG: $10.00

Moments®
Launch Date: April, 1990
Fragrance Type: Parfum: Priscilla Presley's signature fragrance. This fragrance is feminine and romantic, confident and adventurous, with an underlying sense of mystery. *Moments* opens with a chypre floral blending of cassis, orange flower, ylang-ylang and jonquil. As the top notes fade, they give way to a seductive and romantic floral body achieved through a combination of jasmine, rose muguet and tuberose. Finally, anchoring the scent with a warm and alluring base are the essences of sandalwood, patchouli, and moss mingled with musk and vanilla for a lasting effect.
Bottle Design: Created by Mauro Caputo, the heart shaped bottle, frosted glass with a bouquet engraved in bold relief, further underscores the romance of *Moments*.
Package Design: The outer packaging, the color of eggshell, is enlivened with a splash of color—a Matisse inspired floral bouquet.
Pictured Size: .10oz.
Dimensions: 2" h x 1-1/4" w
CPG: $10.00

Fun Facts
on Priscilla Presley
"Priscilla's multifaceted career has included appear-ances in the television series
"THOSE AMAZING ANIMALS" as well as the major role of Jenna Wade in
"DALLAS." She is also the costar in the film series "NAKED GUN,"
"NAKED GUN 2 1/2," AND "NAKED GUN III."
Richard Barrie Fragrances, Inc.

Moments®
Launch Date: April, 1990
Bottle Design: Softly rounded frosted glass.
Package Design: Same as .10oz.
Pictured Size: .08oz.
Dimensions: 1-3/8" h x 1" w
CPG: $5.00

QUINTESSENCE
Div. of Coty, Inc.

Aspen® for Men
"When pulses race...It isn't the Altitude. It's Aspen."
Launch Date: 1989
Fragrance Type: Cologne: Fruity, fresh Fougère. A unique aromatic creation blended with diffusive top notes of lemon and bergamot touched with a freshness of mint. Middle notes of lavender and vetiver enhance the masculine base notes of oakmoss, amber, and musk. A sensuous, powdery and woody base complements this creation.
Pictured Size: .5oz.
Dimensions: 3" h x 1-3/4" w
CPG: $5.00

Caliente®
"Start a Fire."
Launch Date: 1992
Fragrance Type: Cologne: Floral-oriental. Top notes are a fiery blend of sparkling mandarin, neroli, and green fruitiness. Rich spicy, floral middle notes erupt with essences fueled by the embers of woody, musky, ambered, and sweet base notes.
Pictured Size: .125oz.
Dimensions: 2-1/8" h x 3/4" w
CPG: $3.00

Aspen® for Women
Launch Date: 1990
Fragrance Type: Fruity, fresh and floral. A brilliant natural creation capturing the freshness of bergamot and verbena and crisp mountain air with radiant, sparkling floralcy as top notes. Free spirited leafy green notes mingle with subtle hints of fruity notes throughout the balsamic mid notes. A sensuous, powdery, and woody base complements this creation.

Black Orchid®
Launch Date: 1988
Fragrance Type: Perfume: Fresh florals define this exotic fragrance. Top notes of exotic florals and a sparkling, fruity green floral complex are enhanced by light citrus notes. Rich floral heart notes are surrounded by woody, mossy, and ambered base notes.

RALPH LAUREN

Lauren®
Launch Date: 1978
Fragrance Type: Eau de Toilette: Fresh, fruity top notes mingle with floral middle notes and powdery, mossy, and woody base notes.
Pictured Size: .12oz.
Dimensions: 1-3/4" h x 3/4" w
CPG: $11.00

Polo®
Launch Date: 1978
Fragrance Type: Eau de Toilette: Known as the "Fitness Fragrance," it is a crisp, clean, citrus enhanced with woody notes.
Pictured Size: .20oz.
Dimensions: 2-1/8" h x 1-1/8" w
CPG: $8.00

Dare®
Launch Date: 1989
Fragrance Type: Cologne: Classified as floral-chypre this dazzling creation exudes warmth and freshness. Top notes of white florals unfold to reveal spicy, fruity heart notes while warmed by sweet ambered, mossy base notes.

Safari®
Launch Date: May, 1990
Fragrance Type: Eau de Parfum: Floral-Citrusy.
Bottle Design: Created from an antique Victorian bottle. Hand cut crystal. The bottle is presented with a cap that is silver plated with filigree details and inlaid tortoise.
Package Design: A crocodile textured box.
Pictured Size: .25oz.
Dimensions: 1-1/2" h x 1-3/8" w
CPG: $12.00

Safari® for Men®
Launch Date: 1992
Fragrance Type: Eau de Toilette
Pictured Size: .375oz.
Dimensions: 2-1/2" h x 1-1/2" w
CPG: $10.00

RAPHAËL
Raphaël - Paris

Réplique®
Launch Date: 1944 (1946 U.S.A.)
Fragrance Type: Perfume: Fresh, spicy top notes blend elegantly with heart notes that are spicy and floral. Warm, woody, musky base notes that have just a hint of vanilla.
Pictured Size: .06oz.
Dimensions: 1-3/4" h x 1" w
CPG: $15.00

REALM
Erox Corporation

REALM Women™
"An invitation to transcend the senses as you know them, and awaken your sixth sense."
Launch Date: 1992
Fragrance Type: Parfum - A softly beautiful, sophisticated oriental fragrance. It begins with a top note of Sicilian mandarin, Italian cassia, and Egyptian tagettes—a combination both exotic and exhilarating. At the romantic heart of the fragrance are fresh living Peony and Water Lily. Creating a warmly sensual dry-down are woody notes softened and warmed with honey and vanilla.
Bottle Design: The ruby and flint glass bottles are dramatic expressions of the dual nature of *REALM* fragrances. Their red and clear facets capture every flicker of light and shimmer like futuristic jewels, lit from some mysterious source deep inside. Created by world famous bottle designer Pierre Dinand, the *REALM* bottles are dazzling successors to beautiful signature scent bottles of the past.
Pictured Size: .15oz. (Travel Spray)
Dimensions: Photo Courtesy of Erox Corporation
CPG: $60.00

REALM Men™
Launch Date: 1992
Fragrance Type: Eau de Toilette - This fragrance has a traditional, quietly bright scent. It is introduced by crisp, watery top notes of galbanum, bergamot, lavender, and California oranges and mandarin. At the sensual core of the scent is a rich blend of juniper berry, Bois de Rose, and litsea cubea, spiced with ginger. Precious woods like sandalwood and gaiacwood mingle with exotic patchouli to create the essence of deep, long-lasting masculinity in the dry-down.
Bottle Design: The ruby and flint glass bottles are dramatic expressions of the dual nature of *REALM* fragrances, identical to *REALM Women™*. Created by world famous bottle designer Pierre Dinand, the *REALM* bottles are dazzling successors to beautiful signature scent bottles of the past.
Pictured Size: .15oz. (Travel Spray)
Dimensions: Photo courtesy of Erox Corporation
CPG: $60.00

REDKEN LABORATORIES, INC.

Kyenne®
Launch Date: Undetermined
Fragrance Type: Eau de Toilette
Pictured Size: .125oz.
Dimensions: 2" h x 3/4" w
CPG: $8.00

Pique®
Launch Date: Undetermined
Fragrance Type: Perfume
Pictured Size: .125oz.
Dimensions: 1-3/4" h x 1" w
CPG: $5.00

REGINE'S

Parfums Regine's Paris
Inter Parfums

Regine's®
Launch Date: 1989
Fragrance Type: Eau de Toilette: A parfum "De La Nuit" that's alluring, mysterious, seductive, and emanates an uncontrollable energy. Seductive femininity starts the fragrance evening with a top note that is fruity and floral while enticing oriental impressions mingle gently with Egyptian jasmine, blackberry, and a subtle hint of French marigold. The night unfolds with a middle note that explodes with exciting gentle touches of rose and tuberose enlightened by a silky chypre. Traces of patchouli

linger past the midnight hour. With the bottom note, the life of after hours imposes itself. Hidden notes of vanilla and gray amber create a deep sensation—a reminder of unknown moments to come.

Bottle Design: Elegant in packaging, the fragrance is presented in a dreamy, free floating, dancing contour. The top is a carved hat. The design has been developed by Thierry Lecoule, an emerging force in innovative creations.

Pictured Size: .17oz.

Dimensions: 2-1/2" h x 1-1/4" w

CPG: $7.00

REVLON, INC.
Charles Revson

Ajee®
Launch Date: 1994

Fragrance Type: Cologne: Rare and exotic ingredients native to Africa.

Pictured Size: .14oz.

Dimensions: 3/4" h x 1-3/8" w

CPG: $4.00

Charlie®
Launch Date: 1973

Fragrance Type: Fresh, fruity top notes are combined with exotic floral middle notes ending with sweet, powdery, woody base notes.

Pictured Size: .5oz.

Dimensions: 2-1/2" h x 1-3/4" w

CPG: $15.00 - $18.00

Enjoli®
Launch Date: 1978
Fragrance Type: Perfume: Green accords with a hint of floral and fruit create the top notes. Exotic florals blended with powdery base notes complete this fragrance.
Pictured Size: .20oz.
Dimensions: 2" h x 1-1/4" w
CPG: $5.00

Fire and Ice®
"Play with fire. Skate on thin ice."
Launch Date: 1994
Fragrance Type: Perfume: Oriental. Fruity accords with spicy notes. Blends of florals and an exotic mix of amber, woody, and musky notes.
Pictured Size: .16oz.
Dimensions: 2-3/4" h x 1" w
CPG: $4.00

Forever Krystle®
Launch Date: 1988
Fragrance Type: Perfume: A warm and elegant Oriental bouquet with subtle floral undertones.
Pictured Size: .125oz.
Dimensions: 2" h x 1" w
CPG: $6.00

224

Norell®
Norman Norell
Launch Date: 1968
Fragrance Type: Perfume: Fruity and exotic floral top notes are blended with floral middle notes. Powdery florals and mossy, woody notes create the base notes.
Pictured Size: .125oz.
Dimensions: 2" h x 3/4" w
CPG: $5.00

Norell®
Norman Norell
Launch Date: 1968
Pictured Size: .25oz.
Dimensions: 2-1/4" h x 1-1/2" w
CPG: $25.00

Wild Heart®
Launch Date: 1992
Fragrance Type: Cologne: A truly feminine, fruity, floral fragrance with a warm, woody base.
Pictured Size: .15oz.
Dimensions: 2" h x 1-1/4" w
CPG: $3.00

Other Revlon Fragrances

Cerissa®
Launch Date: 1974
Fragrance Type: Sweet-Floral. Fresh, fruity top notes are blended with exotic floral middle notes ending with sweet, balsamic base notes.

Charlie Express®
Launch Date: 1991
Fragrance Type: Floral-Fruity.

Charlie Red®
Launch Date: 1994
Fragrance Type: A bold, fruity sensuous scent that's a few degrees hotter than original Charlie.

Charlie White®
Launch Date: 1995
Fragrance Type: A crisp, floral fragrance that's the romantic new way of Charlie.

Ellen Tracy®
Launch Date: 1992
Fragrance Type: Fresh-Floral.

Guess®
Launch Date: 1990
Fragrance Type: Oriental-Ambered.

Intimate®
Launch Date: 1957
Fragrance Type: Perfume: Top notes are florals with floral, woody middle notes. Base notes are warm, mossy, and ambered.

Jontue®
Launch Date: 1975
Fragrance Type: Perfume: Green accords and fruity notes create the top notes. Middle notes are exotic florals and are blended with woody and ambered base notes.

Lasting®
Launch Date: 1995
Fragrance Type: A classic elegant fragrance that delivers ten hours of consistent wear. *Lasting* is a sparkling fruity-floral scent.

Moon Drops®
Launch Date: 1970
Fragrance Type: Fruity, floral top notes and exotic, sweet floral middle notes are blended with sensual balsamic base notes that will send you to the moon.

ROBERT BEAULIEU
Robert Beaulieu Parfums

Vison®
Launch Date: 1986
Fragrance Type: Eau de Parfum: Floral-Fruity
Pictured Size: .25oz.
Dimensions: 2-3/4" h x 3/4" w
CPG: $6.00

Vison Noir®
Launch Date: Undetermined
Fragrance Type: Eau de Parfum: Floral
Pictured Size: .25oz.
Dimensions: 2-3/4" h x 3/4" w
CPG: $6.00

> **Fun Facts**
> Defining Carnation
> The name carnation was derived from the word coronation.
> Carnations were the chosen flowers of festivals.

ROBERT PIGUET
Robert Piguet - Paris

Fracas®
Launch Date: 1945
Fragrance Type: Parfum: Floral: Leafy green accents and fruity notes delight the top notes. Middle notes are defined by exotic florals and are blended with base notes that are powdery and woody.
Pictured Size: .125oz.
Dimensions: 2" h x 3/4" w
CPG: $7.00

Baghari®
Launch Date: 1950
Fragrance Type: Parfum: Delightful citrusy top notes are blended with classic floral middle notes. Base notes are sweet, powdery, and warm.
Pictured Size: .06oz.
Dimensions: 1" h x 1-1/8" w
CPG: $6.00

Other Piguet Fragrances

bandit®
Launch Date: 1944
Fragrance Type: Chypre-Floral: Herbaceous notes highlight the top notes. Floral middle notes are blended with warm, mossy, and ambered base notes.

Visa®
Launch Date: 1945
Fragrance Type: Chypre

ROCCOBAROCCO

roccobarocco®
Launch Date: 1987
Fragrance Type: Eau de Parfum
Pictured Size: .20oz.
Dimensions: 2-3/8" h x 3/4" w
CPG: $8.00

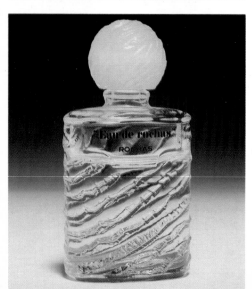

Other Roccobaroco Fragrances

roccobarocco® Uomo
Launch Date: 1989
Fragrance Type: Oriental-Woody.

roccobarocco tre®
Launch Date: 1995

ROCHAS
Marcel Rochas
Rochas Parfums

Audace®
Launch Date: 1930s
Fragrance Type: Perfume
Pictured Size: .07oz.
Dimensions: 2-1/4" h x 3/4" w
CPG: $4.00

Byzance®
"WANTING TO SEDUCE: THE RICHEST, MAGIC AND VOLUPTUOUS DREAM OF A NIGHT"
Launch Date: 1987
Fragrance Type: Eau de Parfum: Semi-oriental based on a wave of fresh and spicy notes. A voluptuous, powerful aroma of Mediterranean gardens.
Bottle Design: A precious, seductive bottle, inspired by Baroque art that evokes a sensuous, rich feminine world.
Package Design: Blue and gold luxurious packaging with golden lace.
Pictured Size: .10oz.
Dimensions: 2" h x 1-1/2" w
CPG: $6.00

"Eau de Rochas"®
"THE QUINTESSENCE OF THE EAU DE TOILETTE FRAÎCHES"
Launch Date: 1970
Fragrance Type: Eau de Toilette: Fresh, light, refined, yet characteristic fragrance made from a selection of ingredients, fruits and flowers from the Mediterranean countries—for the dynamic woman.
Bottle Design: The presentation itself reflects the theme of *freshness* with bottle like a rock crystal.
Package Design: Colors of a running stream.
Pictured Size: .34oz.
Dimensions: 2-3/8" h x 1-1/8" w
CPG: $8.00

Femme®
Launch Date: 1944
Fragrance Type: Perfume: Fruity-chypre, a complex blend with vibrant top notes. It has a rare warmth and quality created by a touch of amber and sandalwood. It is a sophisticated and sensual perfume for a passionate woman.
Bottle Design: As feminine as the fragrance itself, the bottle presentation is based on a gentle "heart shape."
Package Design: A matte and glistening black packaging with a lace pattern inside the box.
Pictured Size: .10oz.
Dimensions: 2" h x 1" w
CPG: $10.00

```
Fun Facts
Femme®
"Lace pattern is inside the box to dress the bottle
as if it were the body of a woman."
Rochas, Paris
```

Madame Rochas®
Launch Date: 1960
Fragrance Type: Perfume: Essentially a floral bouquet, *Madame Rochas* is an exquisite blend of precious essences. The floral top note develops into a harmony of flowers and woody fragrance with animal notes giving an underlying warmth for the distinguished and charming woman.
Pictured Size: .06oz. (round flat)
Dimensions: 1-1/2" h x 1" w
CPG: $25.00

Madame Rochas®
Launch Date: 1960
Bottle Design: The presentation is based on a beautiful 18th century antique bottle. **Package Design:** The packaging design is based on the classic ROCHAS colors: white - red - gold.
Pictured Size: .10oz.
Dimensions: 2-1/2" h x 3/4" w
CPG: $10.00

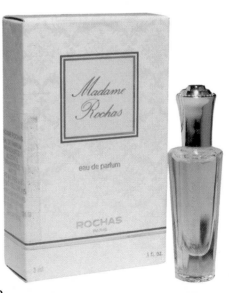

Other Rochas Fragrances

Eau de Rochas® Pour Homme
Launch Date: 1970
Fragrance Type: Chypre-Leathery.

Lumière®
Launch Date: 1984
Fragrance Type: Floral

Macassar®
Launch Date: 1980
Fragrance Type: Chypre-Leathery.

Monsieur Rochas®
Launch Date: 1969
Fragrance Type: Fougère: An exciting, obvious fragrance combining woody notes with spices and a touch of aromatic herbs.

Mystère De Rochas®
Launch Date: 1978
Fragrance Type: Chypre: A well balanced blend of rare essences. This fragrance combines the delicate freshness of cool green citrus with the rich heady sweetness of exotic flowers and the mysterious woody note which give it its character. It is a strange and elusive perfume for a captivating woman.
Bottle Design: An elliptical bottle topped by a polished bordeaux—red cut glass cube.

Tocade®
"Love at First Sight"
Launch Date: 1994
Fragrance Type: Perfume: *Tocade* is an enticing new fragrance of "joie de vivre." Sudden attractions lead to grand passions, fanciful flights lead to sheer delights—infatuations are the spice of life! *Tocade*, a fragrance that embodies life and laughter entwined. Clear, spontaneous, taking flight on a slightly fruity essence of rose together with magnolia blossom. Then bergamot and geranium make their entrance on a base of pure rose. A garden rose, orange, and purple (Turkish rose essence) all make their appearances. Velvety petals release an ample, sweet fragrance with notes of vanilla. Iris notes followed by powdery notes accompany the accord and introduce the rich scents of cedar, benzoin, and rare amber. The floral parade gives way to a powdery note on the skin, leading to warm, intimate notes of amber and musk. A sensual finale!
Bottle Design: Whimsical, playful, yet sensible. To contain *Tocade*, while "expressing boldness with modesty," Serge Mansau chose a humorous approach. With a hint of a smile, the Master of glass gave free rein to virtuosity and took inspiration from the secret techniques of Venetian glass makers. While reflecting the contours that characterize the brand, *Tocade* proclaims a love of color and wittily expresses and infatuation with life. A foot, a body, a head...an almost carnal wrapping for a divinely sensual spirit. Its feminine contours, topped with an amusing little hat, the Tocade bottle is less a provocation than an invitation. It piques curiosity, kindles desire, and surprises with colors and pure lines. A totally contemporary design that has revised the classics to create the most refined of perfumes. Its colored cabochon stopper with long glass stem is a tangible token of its originality. A beautiful way to trace the fragrance all over the skin.
Package Design: *Tocade* expresses "joie de vivre" and sets the tone with cherry red packaging. A luscious red on sensual, coated matte paper. The name is handwritten, the silhouette of the bottle is finely sketched...the packaging spells instant rapture.
Pictured Size: .16oz.
Dimensions: 2-1/2" h x 3/4" w
CPG: $15.00

ROMEO GIGLI
Romeo di Romeo Gigli

Romeo Gigli®
Launch Date: 1991
Fragrance Type: Eau de Parfum:
Soft, fruity, and floral.
Pictured Size: .25oz.
Dimensions: 1-3/4 " h x 1-3/4" w
CPG: $7.00

Other Romeo Gigli Fragrances

Romeo Gigli® per Uomo
Launch Date: April, 1991
Fragrance Type: Oriental-Spicy.

SAKS FIFTH AVENUE

Paradis®
Launch Date: Undetermined
Fragrance Type: Parfum
Pictured Size: .25oz.
Dimensions: 2-1/2" h x 1-1/4" w
CPG: $5.00

Other Saks Fragrances·

Prive®
Launch Date: Undetermined
Fragrance Type: Cologne

SALVADOR DALI
Les Parfums Salvador Dali

Laguna®
Launch Date: 1991

Fragrance Type: Eau de Toilette: Floriental - A marriage of flowers and fruits blended with amber, musk, and vanilla. This fragrance is flowery and feminine, sensual and mysterious, young and dynamic.

Bottle Design: Frosty green bottle with nosed-shaped stopper is filled with the color of the Caribbean Sea—where color and scent communicate.

Package Design: Turquoise packaging is based on Dali's famous canvas painted in 1981—the face of Aphrodite of Knidos.

Pictured Size: .17oz.

Dimensions: 2" h x 1-1/2" w

CPG: $13.00

Fun Facts
On Salvador Dali
"Favorite Color: Absinthe green; Favorite Exercise: Riding up—but not down in an elevator."
Les parfums Salvador Dali

Le Parfum Salvador Dali®
Launch Date: 1986

Fragrance Type: Eau de Toilette: Jasmine and rose with Calabria orange flowers and woodwind notes of cypress, sandalwood, frankincense, myrrh, and incense.

Bottle Design: The retail bottle is patterned after the signed Dali APHRODITE with the same voluptuous lips and Grecian nose.

Package Design: Beige and black packaging frames a miniature of Dali's APHRODITE, true to the colors in the painting, a medley of blue, white, and beige.

Pictured Size: .17oz.

Dimensions: 2" h x 1-1/2" w

CPG: $13.00

Fun Facts
on Salvador Dali®
"About perfume Salvador Dali has written: 'Among the five senses, smell is unquestionably the one that best gives the idea of Immortality.'"
Salvador Dali, Les parfums Salvador Dali

Salvador Dali®

Launch Date: 1987

Fragrance Type: Eau de Toilette Pour Homme:
Woody, Cypress: The dominant chord is rich and
woody blended harmoniously with subtle, sunny,
woody, rustic notes. The warm background is
sweet and ambered.

Bottle Design: Black frosted bottle with mouth
and rounded chin. Above the rounded chin, which
Dali has made a symbol of strength, is a mouth
ready to kiss and be kissed.

Package Design: The case in gray— the gray of
flannel or of an artist's drawing paper—takes up
the theme of Salvador Dali perfume: a frame
around a reproduction of the idea for the bottles
as seen in "The Apparition of the Venus of Knidos."

Pictured Size: .25oz.

Dimensions: 2-1/8" h x 1-1/8" w

SPG: $13.00

Salvador®

Launch Date: 1992

Fragrance Type: Eau de Toilette Pour Homme: A
modern and luminous fragrance that is both spicy
and woody. Top notes sparkle with citrusy notes.
Heart of spices and the essence of rare woods on a
rich, amber background with an aura of incense.

Bottle Design: Partially covered with frost and
hammered in round and regular shapes. The
faceted cap is the color of lapis lazuli veined with
gold.

Package Design: The outside packaging is also
the color of lapis lazuli, and framed with gold, on
which figures a reminder of the chin and mouth
motif.

Pictured Size: .17oz.

Dimensions: 2-1/8" h x 1" w

SPG: $13.00

233

Other Salvador Dali Fragrances

Dalissime®
Launch Date: Spring, 1994 (U.S.A. Launch 1995)
Fragrance Type: Fruity florals and their opal sweetness. Peach and apricot are married to a refined and subtle note akin to the raspberry—that distinctive scent and taste of red fruits glistening with morning dew. A touch of davana, somewhere between plum and prune, and the head notes invade your senses. Transparent, oriental...the heart notes are a delicate touch of litchi suddenly encountering lily, an Indochinese exotic note meeting a cold French note, so well married to Bengal rose and insolent narcissus which brings out the fragrance's character. The transparent and refined litchi notes dominate every level of this masterpiece composition. The end notes are a veritable homage to the mystical Dali: sandalwood and Tonka bean mixed with more sensuous notes such as musk. It is the sandalwood which adds depth and substance to the fragrance. The fragrance is the brilliant achievement of Haarman and Reimer.

Bottle Design: The creation of the new Dalissime bottle was inspired by one of Salvador Dali's 1946 works: "Christmas," which made the cover of Vogue magazine in December of that year. The bottle's design stems from the painting's main element, the arch's column: chin, mouth, and nose topped by a composite capital derived form Corinthian architecture. The bottle is partially sculpted in frosted glass which effectively highlights the famous Dalinian nose and mouth. The master glassmaker is Luigi Bormioli.

Package Design: The box which holds this precious bottle is a complete three dimensional relief replica of "Christmas," obtained through a new fabrication process known as defraction. This new technology was used exclusively for Parfums Salvador Dali, in close collaboration with the cardboard-maker Raffypac. The inspiration for Dalissime's box stems from the painting's main element, represented on the main face, elegantly surrounded by a red and gold trim. The equilibrium of the ruined arch, a kind of geological architecture, was inspired Leonardo da Vinci's work "The Adoration of the Magi." One of the highly original characteristics of Dali's "Christmas" is its stereoscopic effect: when one superimposes the right and left halves of the painting, a woman's face appears. The box's bottom cover is hand-painted in apricot and peach hues with a slight patina to restitute the subtle tints of Roman temple frontispiece.

Eau de Dali®
Launch Date: February, 1995 (U.S.A. Launch 1996)
Fragrance Type: The very fragrance of teen-age youth. As acid as tangerine, pineapple, and lemon, and as soft as ripe peaches and prunes. Eau de Dali carries the freshness of spring's early lilies of the valley, of green leaves crumbled between one's hands, and the blossoming, voluptuousness of rose and jasmine. Its heart has the purity of the ylang-ylang flower and is full of that touch of mystery so well represented by the spicy and powdery iris. Eau de Dali is like a Lolita playing with its trailing scent of vanilla brought to life by amber and sandalwood.

Bottle Design: Its color...pale rose, slightly frosted, as transparent as youth's complexion. Its feel...soft as peach skin. The Eau de Dali bottle is the faithful representation of the world famous mouth and nose so dear to Salvador Dali. This time, however, it is tinted in rose pastel to attenuate the bottle's sensual contour.

Package Design: The tender pink packaging bears in its center a detail of Dali's famous work "Apparition of the Face of Aphrodite of Cnide in a Landscape." The detail is framed by a golden, pink, and white trim. The inscription is in soft pink.

SCULPTURE
Nikos Apostolopoulos
Nikos Parfums Paris

Sculpture®
Launch Date: 1994
Fragrance Type: Perfume: Floral notes with
warm, balsamic base notes.
Pictured Size: .12oz.
Dimensions: 3" h x 3/4" w
CPG: $12.00

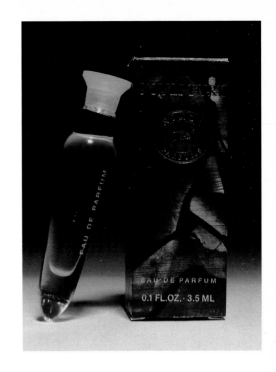

SERGIO TACCHINI

Sergio Tacchini®
Launch Date: 1993 (1994 U.S.A.)
Fragrance Type: Eau de Toilette: Characterized
with green accords for freshness, a blending of
rosemary and bergamot, the zest of lime, and the
warmth of cedar, lavender, and sandalwood.
Pictured Size: .25oz.
Dimensions: 2-1/8" h x 1-1/2" w
CPG: $10.00

Other Sergio Tacchini
Fragrances

Sergio Tacchini Sport Extreme®
Launch Date: 1993
Fragrance Type: Fougère: Unique green and spicy
bouquet enriched with scents of sage, pepper, and
nutmeg, with a woody aroma of amber and musk.

SEVE BALLESTEROS
Severaino Ballesteros

Royal Green®
Launch Date: Undetermined
Fragrance Type: Eau de Toilette: The first
impression of this fragrance is a flash of freshness,
due to its citric notes, full of sun, bergamot, lemon
and mandarin, skillfully combined with a range of
refreshing sea notes, reminiscent of the pure air of
ocean coasts. A green chord evoking the fragrance
of frost on grass, along with notes which are spicy,
fruity, and aromatic, enhance the opening note and
create the heart of this fragrance. We discover the
warmth of its woody notes towards the base of the
fragrance.
Package Design: The box is textured in a natural
green color, reflecting the freshness and the image
of the game played by many: golf. Contrasting with
this background, the coat of arms is in relief,
having been specially designed for Royal Green
and symbolizing the character of the brand; it is
made up of a royal crown, and a green and laurel
ring which envelope the emblem.

Fun Facts
on Seve Ballesteros
"Professional golfer since 1974."
Fragrance Marketing Group

SHULTON, INC.
William Schultz

Desert Flower®
Launch Date: Undetermined
Fragrance Type: Perfume
Pictured Size: .12oz.
Dimensions: 2" h x 3/4" w
CPG: $12.00

Taji®
Launch Date: c1960
Fragrance Type: Perfume Oil
Pictured Size: .12oz.
Dimensions: 1-3/4" h x 3/4" w
CPG: $10.00

Fun Facts
Bewitching Charms
During mediaeval times, male peony seeds were used as charms to ward off witchcraft.

236

SINGLE NOTES
Manufactured Exclusively for Nordstrom

Citrus®
Launch Date: November, 1993
Fragrance Type: Perfume: *Citrus'* appeal is rooted in the intimate association with nature, evoking memories of delicious flavors and astringent sensations. Exhilarating in its fresh, sweet scent, *Citrus* awakens the senses. Notes of fresh, crisp grapefruit, clementine, hyacinth, and touches of apricot begin this invigorating fragrance. The floral heart is composed of gardenia, lily of the valley, jasmine, and orange flower. The dry down is supported with osmanthus, musk, and sandalwood.
Pictured Size: .25oz.
Dimensions: 2-3/8" h x 1" w
CPG: S10.00 (Fragrance Collection Set)

Freesia®
Launch Date: November, 1991
Fragrance Type: Perfume: Light, clean, and simply refreshing, the soft, soothing scent of freesia can add a boost of energy and bring a smile to your face. The long-lasting blooms emit a beautiful fragrance rivaled by few others. The roots are said to possess cleansing properties, thus producing its fresh, pure scent. *Freesia* is a bright, sparkling fragrance, beginning with notes of freesia and splashes of apricot, blending with lily of the valley and marigold to form the heart. The dry down is delicately blended with musk, traces of incense and sandalwood.
Pictured Size: .25oz.
Dimensions: 2-3/8" h x 1" w
CPG: S10.00 (Fragrance Collection Set)

Vanilla®
Launch Date: November, 1994
Fragrance Type: Perfume: From the exquisite orchid family comes the aromatic essence of vanilla. Cultivated in tropical regions, this beautiful flower is the source of a fragrance so wonderful it at once soothes and enlivens the senses. A lively scent begins with vanilla, amber, and touches of fresh raspberry. The dry down is rounded out with creaminess—musk, vanilla, and soft, woody notes.
Pictured Size: .25oz.
Dimensions: 2-3/8" h x 1" w
CPG: S10.00 (Fragrance Collection Set)

White Floral Musk®
Launch Date: November, 1991
Fragrance Type: Perfume: Potent and exotic, musk has long been esteemed as an aphrodisiac. This intoxicating scent historically conjured up implications of romantic delights. Although originally derived from animals, ours is a faithful duplication of this stimulating fragrance, concocted instead from delicate white flowers. This scent begins with crisp, fresh notes of bergamot, mandarin, and galbanum, blended with jasmine, rose, lily of the valley, orange flower, and ylang-ylang to form the heart. The background is rounded out with oakmoss, vetiver, amber, and musk.
Pictured Size: .25oz.
Dimensions: 2-3/8" h x 1" w
CPG: $10.00 (Fragrance Collection Set)

Fun Facts
on The Garden
"Named not for a place, but a person: Dr. Alexander Garden,
an 18th Century botanist from South Carolina."
Nordstrom, Inc.

Other Nordstrom Fragrances

Gardenia®
Launch Date: November, 1991 (revised 1993)
Fragrance Type: Heady and inspiring, gardenia beckons your senses to imagine the lush gardens of the old South. A single fabulous white blossom symbolizes romance; its fragrance speaks of mystery and untold rendezvous. Dewy, fruity notes with hints of violet form the top of this beautiful "Big Floral" fragrance. Gardenia, tuberose, camellia, and linden flower make up the heart. The dry down is supported with notes of musk, wood, and vanilla bean.

Rose®
Launch Date: November, 1991
Fragrance Type: Elusive, delicate, and pure, the rose is the most precious of all potions. Thousands of beautiful blossoms yield mere ounces of essence. Often blended with other fragrances to impart softness and complexity, the rose suggests romance. In aromatherapy, it is prescribed to soothe and relax, as a tonic for depression. The top of this delightful floral scent is a formulation of apricot and sweet leafy green. The middle is a mix of rose, carnation, and lily of the valley, while the dry down is finished with musk, sandalwood, and touches of vanilla.

Fun Facts
Lily White
The story goes: When Undine was bestowed with the kiss
of immortality, her gown "turned lily white."

SMALTO
Francesco Smalto
Parlux Fragrances, Inc.

Francesco Smalto®
"Smalto. You make me Weak."
Launch Date: 1988
Fragrance Type: Eau de Toilette: Fresh Fougère.
Bottle Design: Masculine flacon in smoky gray glass enhanced with a gold logo.
Package Design: Designer Francesco Smalto's signature blue lapis with gold accents and borders.
Pictured Size: .17oz.
Dimensions: 2" h x 1-1/8" w
CPG: $5.00

Molto Smalto®
"Extraordinaire, not Ordinaire."
Launch Date: 1993
Fragrance Type: Eau de Toilette: Warm Aromatic.
Bottle Design: Masculine flacon in matte black glass.
Package Design: Burled wood pattern with chocolate brown accents and gold borders.
Pictured Size: .17oz.
Dimensions: 2" h x 1-1/8" w
CPG: $8.00

Other Smalto Fragrances

Smalto Donna®
Launch Date: 1994
Fragrance Type: Floral-Oriental.

SOCIETY BY BURBERRYS

Society by Burberrys®
Launch Date: March, 1992
Fragrance Type: Parfum: Floral and herbal notes.
Bottle Design: Faceted column-style glass crowned with a ruby-like jewel tone cap and embossed with a silver knight—Burberry's insignia.
Pictured Size: .14oz.
Dimensions: 2-1/2" h x 3/4" w
CPG: $8.00

Other Burberry Fragrances

Burberrys® for Men
Launch Date: 1981
Fragrance Type: Chypre-Leathery.

TETLOW
Henry Tetlow Co.

Blue Moon®
Launch Date: Early 1900s
Pictured Size: .125oz.
Dimensions: 1-3/4" h x 1-1/8" w
CPG: $25.00-$35.00

TIFFANY & CO.

Tiffany® For Men
Launch Date: 1989
Fragrance Type: Cologne: Oriental-Ambered.
Pictured Size: .25oz.
Dimensions: 2-1/2" h x 1-3/8" w
CPG: $13.00 (Not sold individually by Tiffany & Co.)

Tiffany®
Launch Date: 1987
Fragrance Type: Eau de Parfum: Elegant fruity, floral fragrance.
Pictured Size: .25oz.
Dimensions: 1-1/2" h x 2" w
CPG: $15.00 (Not sold individually by Tiffany & Co.)

Trueste®
Launch Date: 1995
Fragrance Type: Eau de Parfum: Fresh, fruity, floral scent.
Pictured Size: .25 oz.
Dimensions: 2-1/4" h x 1-3/4" w
CPG: $25.00 (Not sold individually by Tiffany & Co.)

TITA

Tita Rossi

Tita® de Tita Rossi
Launch Date: 1987
Fragrance Type: Parfum
Pictured Size: .17oz.
Dimensions: 2" h x 2-1/8" w
CPG: $7.00

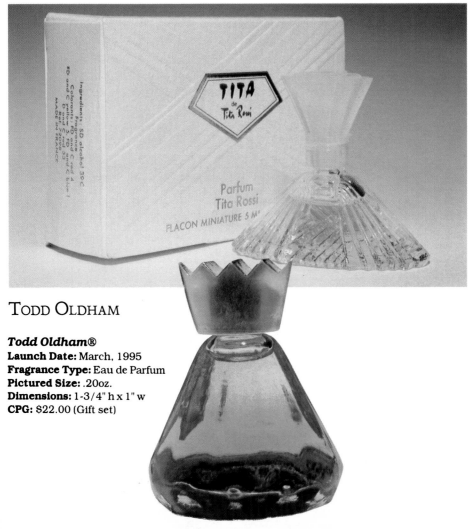

TODD OLDHAM

Todd Oldham®
Launch Date: March, 1995
Fragrance Type: Eau de Parfum
Pictured Size: .20oz.
Dimensions: 1-3/4" h x 1" w
CPG: $22.00 (Gift set)

TRUSSARDI

Trussardi®
Launch Date: 1980
Fragrance Type: Parfum: Chypre-Floral.
Package Design: Lizard-style sheath that bears the Trussardi greyhound emblem.
Pictured Size: .17oz.
Dimensions: 2-1/4" h x 1/4" w
CPG: $6.00

Trussardi® Uomo
Launch Date: 1984
Fragrance Type: Eau de Toilette: Florals, leather, tobacco, and woody notes.
Pictured Size: .17oz.
Dimensions: 2-1/4" h x 1/4" w
CPG: $4.00

Other Trussardi Fragrances

Trussardi Action®
Launch Date: 1989
Fragrance Type: Floral

Trussardi Action® Uomo
Launch Date: 1990
Fragrance Type: Chypre-Leathery.

UGO VANELLI

Ugo Vanelli®
Launch Date: Undetermined
Fragrance Type: Eau de Parfum: Floral bouquet.
Pictured Size: .10oz.
Dimensions: 2-1/4" h x 1" w
CPG: $15.00

ULTIMA II
Charles Revson
Revlon, Inc.

Ciara®
Launch Date: 1973
Fragrance Type: Perfume: The "devastatingly female fragrance" that has been a favorite since its launch in 1973. Ciara is a floral-oriental.
Pictured Size: .125oz.
Dimensions: 2" h x 1" w
CPG: $5.00

Maroc®
Launch Date: 1987
Fragrance Type: Eau de Toilette: Chypre-Floral.
Pictured Size: .125oz.
Dimensions: 1-3/4" h x 1" w
CPG: $5.00

Other Ultima Fragrances

Ciara Femme Fatale®
Launch Date: 1995
Fragrance Type: This floral oriental is a striking sister to the original *Ciara*. *Ciara Femme Fatale* is a sensual, alluring, and sophisticated fragrance.

Head Over Heels®
Launch Date: 1994
Fragrance Type: Perfume: A signature fruity-floral fragrance with a clean, sexy snap.
Package Design: Head Over Heels comes in an absolutely one of a kind bottle. Its unique cap features an upturned pair of legs diving into a frosted bottle of pink fragrance.

UNGARO, PARFUMS
Emanuel Ungaro
Parfums Ungaro, Inc.

DIVA®
Launch Date: 1983
Fragrance Type: Eau de Parfum: *DIVA* is a floral, amber fragrance. Rose, Florentine iris, Egyptian jasmine, Indian tuberose, all interweave with an amber accent followed by woody notes.
Bottle Design: Sculpted crystal bottle.
Pictured Size: .25oz.
Dimensions: 2-1/2" h x 1-1/2" w
CPG: $20.00

SenSo®
Launch Date: 1994
Fragrance Type: Eau de Parfum: Little sister of
DIVA. Fresh top notes sparkling with citrus.
Grapefruit mingled with bergamot. Heart notes
unfold with traditional flowers. Sweet rose, slightly
peppery carnation, and jasmine announce the
sensual base notes.
Pictured Size: .10oz.
Dimensions: 2" h x 1/2" w
CPG: $7.00

Ungaro®
Launch Date: August, 1992
Fragrance Type: Parfum: Fruity, floral, and mossy
Bottle Design: Iris blue bottles and capped with
an emerald green stopper.
Pictured Size: .10oz.
Dimensions: 2" h x 1" w
CPG: $5.00

VALENTINO
Mario Valentino

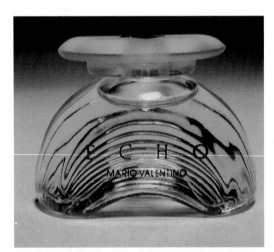

Echo®
Launch Date: 1989
Fragrance Type: Eau de Parfum: Oriental: Spicy
and ambered.
Pictured Size: .17oz.
Dimensions: 1-3/8" h x 2" w
CPG: $12.00

Valentino®
Launch Date: 1977
Fragrance Type: Eau de Parfum: Citrus oils and fruity notes define the top notes while light florals are at the heart of this fragrance. Base notes are floral and mossy.
Pictured Size: .17oz.
Dimensions: 2-1/2" h x 3/4" w
CPG: $10.00

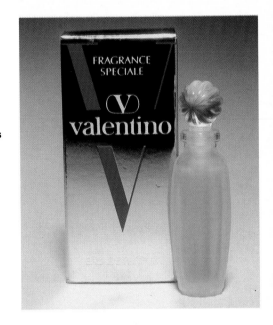

Vendetta®
Launch Date: 1991
Fragrance Type: Eau de Toilette: Floral
Pictured Size: .25oz.
Dimensions: 2-1/2" h x 2-1/2" w
CPG: $7.00

Other Mario Valentino Fragrances

Ocean Rain®
Launch Date: 1990
Fragrance Type: Chypre

VAN CLEEF & ARPELS

First®
Launch Date: 1976
Fragrance Type: Parfum: Fruity top notes blended with elegant florals and woody base notes.
Pictured Size: .17oz.
Dimensions: 2-1/2" h x 1-1/2" w
CPG: $7.00

Gem®
Launch Date: 1988
Fragrance Type: Eau de Toilette: Chypre-Fruity.
Pictured Size: .14oz.
Dimensions: 2-1/8" h x 1-1/4" w
CPG: $5.00

Other Van Cleef & Arpels Fragrances

Miss Arpels®
Launch Date: 1995
Fragrance Type: Fresh and fruity.

Tsar®
Launch Date: 1989
Fragrance Type: Fougère

Van Cleef & Arpels®
Launch Date: 1978
Fragrance Type: Floral-Aldehydic.

Van Cleef® de Van Cleef & Arpels
Launch Date: 1993

VICKY TIEL
Parlux Fragrances, Inc.

Vicky Tiel Sirène®
"Cast the spell..."
Launch Date: March, 1993
Fragrance Type: Eau de Parfum: Floral oriental fragrance.
Bottle Design: Executed by Pierre Dinand. Classic frosted urn silhouette with multiple sculpted goddesses encircling in bas relief.
Package Design: A delicate image of the Roman Goddess of Love on a matte black body. Accents of sunlit yellow and fresh, vibrant peach.
Pictured Size: .17oz.
Dimensions: 2-3/8" h x 3/4" w
CPG: $15.00

Victor

Acqua di Selva®
Launch Date: 1949
Fragrance Type: Eau de Cologne: Fougère
Pictured Size: .20oz.
Dimensions: 2" h x 1-3/8" w
CPG: $4.00

Wall Street®
Launch Date: 1984
Fragrance Type: Eau de Toilette: Fougère-Fresh.
Pictured Size: .20oz.
Dimensions: 2" h x 1-1/2" w
CPG: $4.00

Other Victor Fragrances

Silvestre®
Launch Date: 1946
Fragrance Type: Fougère

V by Victor®
Launch Date: 1972
Fragrance Type: Fougère

Victoria's Secret

Encounter®
Launch Date: 1994
Fragrance Type: Parfum: Floral-oriental. A "sheer" floral that is warm and distinctive without the characteristic sweetness often associated with oriental fragrances.
Pictured Size: .125oz.
Dimensions: 1-3/4" h x 1-1/4" w
CPG: $15.50

Rapture® *(Previous Page)*
Launch Date: 1992
Fragrance Type: Parfum: Floral-oriental. A captivating, sensual, voluptuous fragrance that marries the most sumptuous florals of nature to intoxicating amber and woods.
Pictured Size: .125oz.
Dimensions: 1-1/2" h x 1-1/2" w
CPG: $19.50

Victoria®
Launch Date: 1988
Fragrance Type: Parfum: Victoria is the essence of romantic flowers, tempting fruits, and rich warm woods.
Pictured Size: .125oz.
Dimensions: 1-3/4" h x 1-1/4" w
CPG: $18.50

> **Fun Facts**
> The Passion Flower
> Passion flowers have long been used as an aide for relaxation and sleep.

VOLAGE

Volage®
Launch Date: Undetermined
Fragrance Type: Parfum
Pictured Size: .125oz.

WORTH
Charles Frederick Worth
Les Parfums Worth

Dans la Nuit®
(Into the night)
Launch Date: 1920
(Reintroduced 1985)
Fragrance Type: Perfume: Florals with accents of amber and musk.
Pictured Size: .20oz.
Dimensions: 2-1/4 " h x 1-1/2" w
CPG: $8.00

Je Reviens®
(I will return)
Launch Date: 1932
Fragrance Type: Perfume: Classic floral scent. It is a sophisticated fragrance with fresh green top notes, touches of orange and lemon, mellowing to warm, smoky under notes.
Bottle Design: Boule-shaped and star-studded, bottle design recalls for Jean-Philippe the soft nights and silver skies of his Italian lakes holiday.
Pictured Size: .125oz.
Dimensions: 2-3/4" h x 1-1/8" w
CPG: $10.00

Je Reviens®
Launch Date: 1932
Pictured Size: .125oz.
Dimensions: 2-1/2" h x 1/2" w
CPG: $10.00

Je Reviens®
Launch Date: 1932
Pictured Size: .25oz.
Dimensions: 1-3/4" h x 1-1/2" w
CPG: $12.00

Other Worth Fragrances

Miss Worth®
Launch Date: 1977
Fragrance Type: Perfume: Hints of floral, fruit and greens hi-light the type notes. Floral middle notes blend with sensual powdery and woody base notes.
Bottle Design: Diamond shaped cut glass with same style stopper.

Monsieur Worth®
Launch Date: 1969
Fragrance Type: Aftershave: Distinguished and assertive.

Worth® Pour Homme
Launch Date: 1980
Fragrance Type: After Shave: Exciting and refreshing, lavender, Provence thyme, Morocco artemisia, mint, aniseed, and a hint of pineapple give it sparkle. Juniper berries, lemon, and jasmine make it strong and a fashionable streak of patchouli and sandalwood gives it its subtlety.
Bottle Design: Gray bottle defined by the green liquid of after shave.

249

YVES ROCHER
Yves Rocher France

8e Jour®
Launch Date: 1993
Fragrance Type: Eau de Toilette: Sensuous, exotic floral and spice top notes are blended with middle notes of vibrant florals. Sandalwood, myrrh, and incense create the rich base notes.
Bottle Design: This amber flask is designed to "express the fire within your soul"—an infinite flame.
Pictured Size: .25oz.
Dimensions: 2-1/2" h x 1-3/4" w
CPG: $5.00

Antarctic®
Launch Date: Undetermined
Fragrance Type: Eau de Toilette
Pictured Size: .25oz.
Dimensions: 2-3/8" h x 1-3/4" w
CPG: $4.00

Cantata®
Launch Date: 1995
Fragrance Type: Eau de Toilette: Top notes of rose, jasmine, and iris. Heart notes of osmanthus, cinnamon, and nectarine. Base notes of cedar, sandalwood, and caramel.
Pictured Size: .25oz.
Dimensions: 2" h x 1" w
CPG: $6.00

Cap Nature®
Launch Date: 1995
Fragrance Type: Eau de Toilette: Fruit Rouge
Pictured Size: .25oz.
Dimensions: 1-3/8" h x 1-3/8" w
CPG: $6.00

Cléa®
Launch Date: 1981
Fragrance Type: Eau de Toilette: Aldehyde-Floral.
Pictured Size: .5oz.
Dimensions: 3" h x 1-3/8" w
CPG: $4.00

Désir de Nature®
Launch Date: 1994
Fragrance Type: Eau de Toilette: Top notes are a bouquet of florals with sparkling fruity notes. Fragrance heart explodes with more exuberant florals while base notes are of exotic woods.
Bottle Design: Leaf-like shape with raised veins. Light green glass with light green plastic stopper. Lettering is scripted dark green on glass.
Pictured Size: .16oz.
Dimensions: 2-3/8" h x 1" w
CPG: $5.00

Ispahan®
Launch Date: 1982
Fragrance Type: Eau de Toilette: Exotic florals with a hint of citrus notes top off this fragrance whose middle notes are spicy and floral. Base notes are jasmine and patchouli.
Bottle Design: Rich, midnight blue with gold band around top and lettering.
Pictured Size: .5oz.
Dimensions: 2-1/8" h x 1-3/8" w
CPG: $6.50

Magnolia®
Launch Date: 1983
Fragrance Type: Eau de Toilette: An enticing blossoming bouquet of florals with base notes of musk and black currant.
Pictured Size: .5oz.
Dimensions: 2-1/2" h x 1-3/4" w
CPG: $5.00

Milrose®
Launch Date: Undetermined
Fragrance Type: Eau de Toilette
Pictured Size: .25oz.
Dimensions: 2-1/8" h x 1-1/8" w
CPG: $4.00

Nuit D'Orchidee®
Launch Date: Undetermined
Fragrance Type: Eau de Toilette Concentre
Pictured Size: .25oz.
Dimensions: 2" h x 1-1/4" w
CPG: $8.00

Orchidee®
Launch Date: Undetermined
Fragrance Type: Eau de Toilette: Experience the aura of a lush tropical paradise with exotic florals and lingering base notes of rich vanilla.
Pictured Size: .25oz.
Dimensions: 2" h x 1-1/4" w
CPG: $5.00

Pivoine®
Launch Date: Undetermined
Fragrance Type: Eau de Toilette: This mesmerizing scent of blossoms mingled with rich, subtle, and warm spices.
Pictured Size: .25oz.
Dimensions: 2" h x 1-1/2" w
CPG: $4.00

Soleil Bleu®
Launch Date: Undetermined
Fragrance Type: Eau Parfumante
Pictured Size: .25oz.
Dimensions: 2-1/2" h x 1-1/4" w
CPG: $3.00

Venice®
Launch Date: 1986
Fragrance Type: Eau de Toilette: Seductive and elegant, Venice is made up of warm, alluring notes of rich florals and a base note of vanilla.
Bottle Design: Jewel notes of crimson and gold. Named for the Italian city of lovers.
Pictured Size: .25oz.
Dimensions: 3-1/8" h x 1" w
CPG: $6.00

Vie Privée®

Launch Date: 1989

Type: Eau de Toilette: Fresh, floral scent of a pure white bouquet. Top notes are narcissus with heart notes of freesia, white rose, and white lilac. Base note is white iris. Fragrance creation was inspired to "reflect hopes and dreams from deep within your heart."

Bottle Design: Exquisite sea-green frosted glass bottle with white flower pedal stopper.

Pictured Size: .25oz.

Dimensions: 2" h x 1-3/4" w

CPG: $7.00

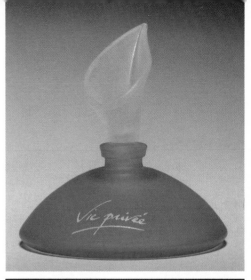

Other Yves Rocher Fragrances

Aztek®

Launch Date: 1994

Fragrance Type: Herbaceous, spicy, and woody.

Chevrefeuille®

Launch Date: Undetermined

Fragrance Type: Delicate floral fragrance with top notes of lemon and orange, middle notes of honeysuckle, and base notes of jasmine.

Trimaran®

Samarkande®

YSL

Yves Saint Laurent

Yves Saint Laurent Parfums Corp.

Kouros®

Launch Date: 1981

Fragrance Type: Eau de Toilette: Fougère: Woody and ambered.

Pictured Size: .34oz.

Dimensions: 2-3/4" h x 1-3/8" w

CPG: $8.00

> **Fun Facts**
> Kouros®
> First Men's Fragrance

Opium® (Previous Page)
Launch Date: 1977
Fragrance Type: Parfum: Oriental, spicy top notes mingle with spicy, floral heart notes and warm, sweet, balsamic base notes for an addictive scent.
Pictured Size: .12oz.
Dimensions: 1-1/2" h x 1-1/8" w
CPG: $10.00

Paris®
Launch Date: 1983
Fragrance Type: Eau de Toilette: Fresh, floral top notes are blended into radiant floral middle notes. Base notes are soft and powdery.
Pictured Size: .25oz.
Dimensions: 1-1/2" h x 1-1/4" w
CPG: $10.00

Rive Gauche®
Launch Date: 1971
Fragrance Type: Parfum: Floral-Aldehydic: Peach notes and leafy greens top this fragrance off. Middle notes are elegant florals blended with mossy, feminine base notes.
Pictured Size: .125oz.
Dimensions: 2" h x 3/4" w
CPG: $3.00

Fun Facts
Y®
Yves Saint Laurent's first fragrance.

Y®
Launch Date: 1964
Fragrance Type: Parfum: Chypre: Fruity, classic florals blended with warm, woody notes.
Pictured Size: .1oz.
Dimensions: 1-3/4" h x 1" w
CPG: $3.00

Y®
Launch Date: 1964
Pictured Size: .13oz.
Dimensions: 2-1/4" h x 3/4" w
CPG: $11.00

Other YSL Fragrances

Champagne®
Launch Date: 1994
Fragrance Type: Eau de Toilette: This fruity, floral, chypre is touched with a note of "living" nectarine.

ZEENAT AMAN
Parfums Zeenat Aman Paris

Zeenat®
Launch Date: Undetermined
Fragrance Type: Eau de Toilette
Pictured Size: .25oz.
Dimensions: 2-3/8" h x 2" w
CPG: $8.00

ZENUE
Div. of Hydrotech Laboratories

Frederique®
"THE SPIRIT OF A WOMAN"
Launch Date: September, 1994
Fragrance Type: Cologne: Inspired by Dutch born
international model, Frederique. *Frederique*
captures the spirit of a woman: sensual, confident
and provocative. The new fragrance by **Zenue** is a
modern, transparent floral with a classic twist.
The top note is exhilarating, fresh, transparent and
dewy. The heart is a big floral bouquet, made of
signature absolutes (iris, mimosa, and orange
flower) that give incredible richness and depth.
"Enfleurage 2000," an exclusive technology,
captures the scent and complete impression of a
flower in bloom, creating a delicate blend. The
drydown approaches warmth in an entirely new
way...precious amber, dry woods, and a veil of
smooth tuberose flower are blended together,
creating a lighter, more intimate warmth. The
fragrance was designed and marketed by Sutton
Pina Associates for Hydrotech Labs.
Bottle Design: The frosted bottle and brushed
silver cap mimic the dewy freshness of the
fragrance. The signature logo is individualistic and
organic in feel.
Package Design: Clean, simple, sophisticated, the
Frederique package is contemporary. The second-
ary packaging is cylindrical in shape and all
packaging is recyclable.
Pictured Size: .25oz.
Dimensions: 3" h x 3/4" w
CPG: $5.50

Frederique

ZINO DAVIDOFF
Parfums Davidoff

Cool Water®
Launch Date: 1988
Fragrance Type: Eau de Toilette: Spicy, floral blends come together with soft, powdery base notes.
Bottle Design: Cool water blue glass.
Pictured Size: .10oz.
Dimensions: 1-3/4" h x 1" w
CPG: $7.00

Zino Davidoff®
Launch Date: 1986
Fragrance Type: Eau de Toilette: Woody, powdery notes create this masculine fragrance.
Bottle Design: Deep brown glass bottle.
Pictured Size: .25oz.
Dimensions: 2-1/8" h x 1-1/8" w
CPG: $7.00

Fun Facts
Author's Final Thought

With all the fancies and frills that are provided us today as remedies and recipes for cosmetic beauty, none compare to following—author unknown.

"A youthful looking, graying Quaker lady was asked what she used
to preserve her appearance. She replied calmly:
I use for the lips, truth;
for the voice, prayer;
for the eyes, pity;
for the hand, charity;
for the figure, uprightness;
for the heart, love."

BIBLIOGRAPHY

Haarman & Reimer. *The H & R Fragrance Guide: Femine Notes. Fragrances on the International Market.* West Germany, Johnson Publications Limited, 1984.

Haarman & Reimer. *The H & R Book of Perfume: Understanding Fragrances. Origin, History, Development, Meaning.* West Germany, Johnson Publications Limited, 1984.

Lefkowith, Christie, Mayer. *The Art of Perfume: Discovering and Collecting Perme Bottles.* New York, Thames and Hudson, 1994.

MacNicol, Mary. *Flower Cookery.* New York, The Macmillian Company, 1967.

Madsen, Axel. *CHANEL: A Woman of Her Own.* New York, Henry Holt and Company, 1990.

Morris, Edwin T. *The Story of Perfume from Cleopatra to Chanel.* United States of America, Charles Scribner's Sons, 1984.

North, Jacquelyne Y., Jones. *Commercial Perfume Bottles.* Pennsylvania, Schiffer Publishing, Ltd., 1987.

O'Higgins, Patrick. *Madame: An Intimate Biography of helena Rubinstein.* New York, The Viking Press, 1971.

Sloan, Jean. *Perfume and Scent Bottle Collecting.* Illinois, Wallace-Homestead Book Company, 1986.

Index and Cross Reference